D0871711

BOOK OF MORMON:
A History of Real People in Real Places

Terrence J. O'Leary

Copyright © 2020 by Terrence J. O'Leary.

All rights reserved. No part of this publication may be reproduced, distributed or transmit-
ted in any form or by any means, including photocopying, recording, or other electronic
or mechanical methods, without the prior written permission of the publisher, except in
the case of brief quotations embodied in critical reviews and certain other noncommercial
uses permitted by copyright law. For permission requests, write to the publisher, addressed
"Attention: Permissions Coordinator," at the address below.

Book of Mormon: A History of Real People in Real Places

Author: Terrence J. O'Leary

Cover: Robert W. O'Leary

ISBN 978-1-09830-563-5

DEDICATION

To my mother, Dorothy E. O'Leary, who shared her strength, dedication, love, and faith to provide a foundation upon which I could grow.

And I exhort you to remember these things: for the time speedily cometh that ye shall know that I lie not, for ye shall see me at the bar of God: and the Lord God will say unto you, Did I not declare my words unto you, which was written by this man, like as one crying from the dead?

—Moroni 10:22 (10:27)

Evidence is provided here

to show that the events described

in the Book of Mormon

actually happened.

The people mentioned in the Book of Mormon

were real people.

The book is literally true and

the trials, labors, and testimonies of those people

are also true.

When seen in this way, the Book of Mormon

becomes a strong testimony that

JESUS CHRIST LIVES!

TABLE OF CONTENTS

PREFACE

I was baptized at the age of eight and became a member of the Reorganized Church of Jesus Christ of Latter Day Saints (now known as the Community of Christ). I had a certain fascination with the Book of Mormon in my youth. However, I was uncomfortable with some of the ideas regarding geography and some scriptural interpretations.

I gained some research skills during my college years. Many years later after my retirement, I had time to do some serious research on both church history and the Book of Mormon.

My science background has strongly benefitted my research on the Book of Mormon. In the process, I gained scriptural insights based on the cultural context within the time and places where these people lived. Over the years, I found myself putting the pieces together in such a way that the book became very real.

A couple of years ago, I presented a series of lectures on varying aspects of the Book of Mormon. After several presentations, I was strongly encouraged to write this book.

I also wrote this book, in part, for those who know very little about the Book of Mormon. I have included elements of the narrative so that those unfamiliar with the Book of Mormon can better understand the context. It is an attempt to bring to life the events described.

ACKNOWLEDGMENTS

I must first give credit to my mother who had the strength to raise two very rambunctious boys by herself. During my youth, we regularly attended church services at the Reorganized Church of Jesus Christ of Latter Day Saints Christ (now known as the Community of Christ).

I must give credit to B.A. and Marcene Howard who were instrumental in reigniting my interest in church history, and the Book of Mormon. I must also acknowledge Verneil Simmons who subsequently sparked a deeper interest in me for the Book of Mormon.

I must also give credit to Don Rose and Charles Presley who were very instrumental in my faith journey.

I have given several presentations regarding my research on the Book of Mormon. From that, I must now give credit to the many people who have encouraged me to write this book.

I must also acknowledge my wife for her patience for the many hours spent on the computer as I worked my way through all the research, writing, and editing.

There is not enough room to give credit and thanks to all those who have influenced my life and supported this effort. For all of them, *thank you*!!!

I must give the greatest credit, however, to the Lord. On many occasions, I have felt led by the Holy Spirit when I was putting the pieces together of what figuratively amounts to a giant jigsaw puzzle. As you read the following chapters, I only ask for your serious consideration that the Book of Mormon is a historic record containing the testimonies of real people.

NOTES ON QUOTATIONS FROM THE BOOK OF MORMON

RLDS refers to the Community of Christ / Reorganized Church of Jesus Christ of Latter Day Saints with headquarters in Independence, Missouri.

LDS refers to the Church of Jesus Christ of Latter-day Saints with headquarters in Salt Lake City, Utah.

The Book of Mormon has gone through numerous editions since it was first published in 1830. The original edition divided each book into chapters; however, the chapters were not divided into verses. A few early editions numbered the paragraphs (1852 LDS European edition and 1874 RLDS edition). In 1879, the LDS Church established a different format. The text was divided into smaller chapters, and each chapter was divided into verses—for ease of reference. In 1903, the RLDS Church gained custody of the original printer's manuscript. This resulted in the publication of the 1908 RLDS edition which corrected a few typesetting errors made in 1830. This edition kept the same chapter divisions as the 1830 edition but divided the chapters into verses. As a result, the current RLDS editions have fewer chapters and more verses per chapter as compared to the current LDS editions. For example, 1 Nephi is divided into seven chapters in the 1830 and RLDS editions while 1 Nephi in the LDS edition is divided into twenty-two chapters.

Except as noted, all quoted excerpts from the Book of Mormon in this work are from the 1830 edition. In each case, a reference is provided to the RLDS edition followed by a bracketed reference to the LDS edition.

INTRODUCTION

The Book of Mormon was first published in 1830. The coming forth of this book was described as a series of miraculous circumstances that involved an angel of the Lord, a record on metal plates, and a perplexing method of translation. Some accept it on faith while others consider the circumstances too far-fetched.

The profound content of the Book of Mormon is foundational to the faith of millions of people. Among those who also hold the Doctrine and Covenants as scriptural, the importance of the message was provided.

> *...the Book of Mormon, which contains a record of a fallen people, and the fullness of the gospel of Jesus Christ to the Gentiles, and to the Jews also, which was given by inspiration, and is confirmed to others by the ministering of angels, and is declared unto the world by them, proving to the world that the Holy Scriptures are true.*
>
> —Doctrine and Covenants 17:2c–e (20:7–10)

When understood to be literally true, the Book of Mormon has made the gospel, as described in the Bible, much larger, more real, and more relevant. This work is an attempt to provide correlations between the events described in the Book of Mormon with a variety of sources. Those sources include the Bible, the history of ancient cultures, archaeology, geography, geology, and oceanography. The evidence provided is intended to substantiate the events described in the Book of Mormon.

There are varied ideas regarding the geography involved in these events. When the Book of Mormon was first published, nothing was known of many early civilizations. As a result, some believed that everything recorded in the Book of Mormon took place in North America where the Book of Mormon plates were found.

People from varying cultures, long before Columbus, had discovered the Americas. Some people migrated across the Bering Strait from Asia. This included members of the Clovis culture of North America—predating the earliest people mentioned in the Book of Mormon by thousands of years. Prehistoric migrations from other parts of the world to the Americas is also evident.

The people described in the Book of Mormon did not live inside a giant fortress. Over the eons of time, it is likely that many small groups quietly migrated across lands or seaward carrying their culture with them. They may have encountered other populations and cultures and were absorbed by them. All of this adds to the confusion regarding the geography of the Book of Mormon. However, all the events described in the Book of Mormon have many parallels in the histories of the Mesoamerican Olmec and Maya.

The Book of Mormon focuses on the histories of three groups of people who came to the Americas. The Book of Mormon is a record of their histories. What follows is a brief orientation to these people.

JAREDITES

The Jaredites were a group of friends who were led by the brother of Jared away from a Great Tower at the time of the confusion of tongues. He was the spiritual leader of his family, his friends, and their families. Their journey brought them across the ocean to the Americas. As the population grew, political fighting waxed and waned. After many centuries, a final battle brought their culture to an end. Their history is evidenced within the remains of the Olmec civilization.

NEPHITES VS. LAMANITES

A spiritual leader, Lehi, led his family out of Jerusalem during the first year of the reign of King Zedekiah. At the time of Lehi's departure, he had four sons, Laman, Lemuel, Sam, and Nephi. They brought with them a set of brass plates containing the scriptures of that day. Another family with daughters joined them so that each of the sons had a wife. This group traveled across the ocean. After their arrival in the Americas, Lehi passed away. Animosity among the brothers forced them to separate into two groups. One group was led by Laman; hence, they became known as the Lamanites. They were generally hard-hearted and from the beginning, very threatening to their younger brothers. The other group was led by Nephi, hence they were known as Nephites. He was a spiritual leader guided by the Lord. As the centuries passed, their descendants had to flee from the Lamanites. The hostility between the Nephites and Lamanites would continue intermittently for many years.

MULEKITES

The conquering of Jerusalem by King Nebuchadnezzar and the removal of Zedekiah from the throne marked the beginning of the story of the Mulekites. This third group appears to have included at least one child of King Zedekiah. Apparently, with the help of others, this child was able to escape and eventually ended up in the Americas. His descendants became known by us as the Mulekites. Many years later, those descendants discovered the last survivor of the final battle among the Jaredites.

When the Nephites fled from the warlike Lamanites, they discovered the Mulekites, who then became numbered among the Nephites.

THEY CAME TO KNOW CHRIST

Prophecies and signs were given to the Nephites, so they knew of the time of Christ's birth and death. They were then visited by the risen Christ who expounded the same gospel that He had taught to his followers in the Holy Land. After His visit, the people lived in peaceful harmony for many years. However, eventually, greed, jealousy and a thirst for power began to take hold. The people again separated into groups, primarily as Nephites versus Lamanites.

A RECORD OF THESE PEOPLE

Mormon, a Nephite, lived during a time when faith in the Lord among almost all of the Nephites had waned. The animosities climaxed in a war in which they had to constantly defend themselves from the aggressive Lamanites. Near the end, Mormon had gathered the records of his people and wrote a summary of the history of his people. This abridgment was engraved on golden plates. He was able to hide the original records entrusted to him by the Lord and gave his son his abridgment of their history. A short time later, Mormon was killed in one of the final battles. In the end, the Nephite culture was destroyed.

Mormon's son, Moroni, finished the abridgment, added a summary of the history of the Jaredites and his own thoughts. Moroni hid the plates in a place where they would be found about 1,400 years later by Joseph Smith. With the Lord's help, Joseph Smith was able to translate those plates.

Some people see the Book of Mormon as nineteenth Century fiction. Some see it as inspired but dismiss it as a historic document. However, as time has passed, although the Book of Mormon has not changed, the evidence supporting it has grown. It is here that I wish that those who read this book will see the Book of Mormon as literally true—describing real people who lived in real places.

There is a promise given to those who would read the Book of Mormon:

> *Behold, I would exhort you that when ye shall read these things, if it be wisdom in God that ye should read them, that ye would remember how merciful the Lord hath been unto the children of men, from the creation of Adam, even down until the time that ye shall receive these things, and ponder it in your hearts. And when ye shall receive these things, I would exhort you that ye would ask God, the Eternal Father, in the name of Christ, if these things are not true; and if ye shall ask with a sincere heart, with real intent, having faith in Christ, and he will manifest the truth in you, by the power of the Holy Ghost; and by the power of the Holy Ghost, ye may know the truth of all things.*

—Moroni 10:3–5 (10:3–5)

CHAPTER 1:

JAREDITE JOURNEY
TO THE PROMISED LAND

Ether, one of the last surviving Jaredites, summarized the history of his people. His record was subsequently found and translated by the Nephites. As Moroni finished the record that we call the Book of Mormon, he included his abbreviated version of Ether's account. Moroni admitted that his abridgment was not a "hundredth part" of what had been left by Ether (Ether 6:108 [15:33]).

We are introduced to the Jaredites at the Great Tower during the confusion of tongues.

> *...the Lord confounded the language of the people, and swear in his wrath that they should be scattered upon all the face of the earth; and according to the word of the Lord the people were scattered. And the brother of Jared, being a large and a mighty man, and being a man highly favored of the Lord; for Jared his brother said unto him, Cry unto the Lord, that he will not confound us that we may not understand our words.*
>
> —Ether 1:7–8 (1:33–34)

The Lord granted that request. Then Jared asked his brother to ask the Lord for the same favor for their friends.

And it came to pass that the brother of Jared did cry unto the Lord, and the Lord had compassion upon their friends, and their families also, that they were not confounded.

—Ether 1:11 (1:37)

Jared again asked his brother to plead with the Lord to know if they were to move to a new place and, if so, where. The Lord told the brother of Jared,

Go to and gather together thy flocks, both male and female, of every kind; and also of the seed of the earth of every kind, and thy family¹ and also Jared thy brother and his family; and also thy friends and their families, and the friends of Jared and their families.

—Ether 1:16 (1:41)

What follows is an attempt to trace their route by combining clues from the Book of Mormon with a little bit of geography, oceanography and ancient stories.

THE GREAT TOWER AT UR

Where was the starting point of their journey? The Bible states that Babel was the location of the confusion of tongues (Gen. 11:6–9). The term "Babel" is similar to a Jewish word that simply means "confused." That is why it was called "Babel." It was a tower of confusion.

---

1   A typesetting error in the 1830 edition of the Book of Mormon mistakenly referred to the brother of Jared gathering his "families," implying that he was a polygamist. This error was perpetuated through multiple editions. The error was subsequently discovered many years later when comparisons were made with the original handwritten printer's manuscript. It was then corrected in the 1908 RLDS edition. Not all subsequent editions have corrected the error.

A legend about a tower and the confusion of tongues was recorded in ancient Sumeria. A reference, found on a clay tablet, described a myth in which an irate God altered man's speech. A translation from that clay tablet informs us that:

> *...Enki, the lord of abundance, (whose) commands are trustworthy, The lord of wisdom, who understands the land, The leader of the gods, Endowed with wisdom.... Changed the speech in their mouths, [brought(?)] contention into it, into the speech of man that (until then) had been one.*[2]

Ur is located near the mouth of the Tigris and Euphrates Rivers at the northern end of the Persian Gulf. Excavations at Ur have revealed the remains of a stepped pyramid, ziggurat, or "tower." The cuneiform writing on the associated clay tablet supports the idea that the actual "tower" where the confusion of tongues took place was a ziggurat in Ur.

Ur had flourished for about a thousand years before the famous Ziggurat was built. One king of note was Ur-Nammu (2047–2030 B.C.). He was responsible for undertaking the construction of a great Ziggurat to the city's patron deity, Nanna the Moon God.[3] There was a rapid decline of Ur's size and influence by 2000 B.C.[4] Perhaps this decline, in part, may relate to the scattering of the population due to

---

2   S. N. Kramer. "The 'Babel of Tongues': A Sumerian Version." *Journal of the American Oriental Society*, Vol. 88.1, 1968. p. 111.

3   Dr. Senta German. "Ziggurat of Ur." Khan Academy <https://www.khanacademy.org/humanities/ancient-art-civilizations/ancient-near-east1/sumerian/a/ziggurat-of-ur> 10 Sep 2019.

4   S. N. Kramer, Ph.D., and E. I. Gordon, Ph.D. "Ur," Microsoft® Encarta® Online Encyclopedia 2000. <http://autocww.colorado.edu/~toldy2/E64ContentFiles/ArchaeologyAndExcavations/Ur.html> 10 Sep 2019.

the confusion of tongues. Based on the above, the dispersion from Ur probably occurred between 2100 and 2000 B.C.

JAREDITE ROUTE ACROSS ASIA

The Valley of Nimrod

As directed by the Lord, the brother of Jared brought his family, his friends and their families together. The Lord then told the brother of Jared to lead them north to the Valley of Nimrod.

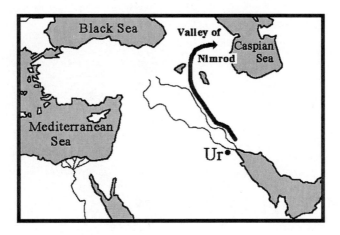

And it came to pass that when they did come down into the valley of Nimrod, the Lord came down and talked with the brother of Jared; and he was in a cloud, and the brother of Jared saw him not. And it came to pass that the Lord commanded them that they should go forth into the wilderness, yea, into that quarter where there never had man been.

—Ether 1:25–26 (2:4–5)

Going from the Valley of Nimrod into an uninhabited land meant they must have traveled eastward. Lands to the north, south, and west were known to be already populated.

> *And it came to pass that they did travel in the wilderness,*
> *and did build barges, in the which they did cross many*
> *waters, being directed continually by the hand of the Lord.*
>
> —Ether 1:28 (2:6)

If they started from the Valley of Nimrod they could have crossed the Caspian Sea and eventually finished by floating down the Yellow River. However, the need to build barges when crossing "*many waters*" in Central Asia may seem implausible. Today it is mostly desert. However, Raphael Pumpelly theorized that much of the early Asian civilization lived near multiple lakes, remnants of the last glacial ice age.

> *The last great change over the Tarim basin* [western
> China] *has been one of desiccation* [dryness]. *Of this, we*
> *have both physiographic and historic records, which tell*
> *that it became serious about a thousand years ago when*
> *some hundreds of cities were overwhelmed by sand. Some*
> *of these ruins were excavated by Stein, and Mr. Pumpelly*
> *found mention of them in Chinese literature in the impe-*
> *rial archives of Pekin. It is also believed there were then*
> *expansive bodies of water of which* [Lake] *Lob-nor and*

other shrunken lakes and brackish tarns [ponds] *are the withering survivals* [of dried-up lakes].[5]

Those large lakes would explain why the Jaredites, about 4,000 years ago, had to build barges to "cros*s many waters.*"

A Mountain Removed

During the Jaredite trek across Asia, an amazing event occurred. Moroni wrote that:

> ...*the brother of Jared said unto the mountain Zerin, Remove, and it was removed And if he had not faith, it would not have moved; wherefore thou workest after that men have faith...*
>
> —Ether 5:30–31 (12:30).

Certainly, such an event in history as the miraculous removal of a mountain would have been remembered. Interestingly, Chairman Mao once related the following Chinese fable.

> *The foolish man's house faced south and two great mountains...obstructed the way. He and his sons...began to dig up the mountains. A wise old man saw them and said it was impossible for four men to dig up two big mountains. The foolish man replied, "When I die my sons will carry on and when they die there will be grandsons and their sons...and so on to infinity. Why can't we clear them*

---

5   Raphael Pumpelly, ed. *Explorations in Turkestan, Expedition of 1904: Prehistoric Civilizations of Anau, Origins, Growth, and Influence of Environment.* v. 2. Washington, D.C.: Carnegie Institution of Washington. 1908. <https://books.google.com/books?id=74kzlWWnNOQC&pg=PA286&lpg=PA286&dq> 20 May 1918. p. 286.

away?" The foolish man went on digging, unshaken...God
was moved by this and sent down two angels who carried
the mountains away on their backs.[6]

A famous pass in the Altai mountain range is known as the Dzungarian Gate. It is a valley that is more than forty miles long. It is the only pass through the eastern end of that mountain range. The ancient silk road went through this pass. Based on the description in the Book of Mormon, some believe that "*This miracle is believed to have happened at the remarkable pass known today as the Dzungarian* Gate."[7]

En Route Across Asia

Behold, O Lord, thou hast smitten us because of our iniq-
uity, and hath driven us forth, and for this many years we
have been in the wilderness; nevertheless, thou hast been
merciful unto us.

—Ether 1:64 (3:3)

After the Jaredites left the Great Tower, an unknown number of years would pass as they trekked across the Asian continent to the shore of a great sea. If they encountered the Yellow River during their journey, it would have provided a constant source of water along with an easier route to follow while floating on their barges. Following the river to its mouth would have brought them to the Shandong Peninsula.

---

6   Louis Heren. *China's Three Thousand Years: The Story of a Great Civilization.* New York: Macmillan Publishing Company, 1974. p. 64.

7   Glenn A. Scott. *Voices from the Dust: New Light on an Ancient American Record.* Marceline, MO: Walsworth Publishing Co., 2002. p. 28.

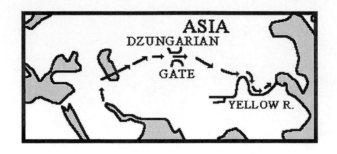

...it came to pass that the Lord did bring Jared and his brethren forth even to that great sea which divideth the lands. And as they came to the sea, they pitched their tents...and they...dwelt in tents upon the seashore for the space of four years.

—Ether 1:36–37 (2:13)

PREPARING THE BARGES

After four years, the Lord told the brother of Jared:

...Go to work and build, after the manner of barges which ye have hitherto built. And it came to pass that the brother of Jared did go to work, and also his brethren, and built barges after the manner which they had built, according to the instructions of the Lord. And they were small, and they were light upon the water; and they were built after a manner that they were exceeding tight; even that they would hold water like unto a dish...

—Ether 1:43–45 (2:16–17)

The barges were described as the length of a tree. When closed, the top, bottom, and sides were all watertight *"like unto a dish."* The use of the term "*barges*" is interesting, for that would seem to imply a lack of sails. Many ancient Egyptian barges did not have sails. The anticipation of heavy seas would also discourage their use.

Describing the barges as light upon the water suggests that they did not draft deep into the water when empty. That would make them capable of carrying sufficient cargo for their journey.

Ancient Egyptian barges navigated by using a rudder and oars. If oars were used in this case, they would have to be mounted from the top deck to retain watertight integrity below. I am not trying to imply that the Jaredites rowed their way across the Pacific Ocean. Connecting these barges together while in heavy seas would doom them to catastrophic collisions. The rudder and oars may have been necessary so they could remain safely within sight of each other while at the same time avoiding collisions. The rudder could also be used to keep the barges aligned into the waves rather than allowing a large wave to hit broadside and risk being capsized. All of this would have been done while being guided by the Lord in this journey. During very heavy seas, when they would have to seal themselves inside, the oars would be tied down and the rudders tied in place. They would then have to depend upon the Lord to keep them safe until the storm passed.

A Hole in the Top and Bottom

The brother of Jared then went to the Lord fearing that they would suffer and die from lack of fresh air in the barges.

> *And the Lord said unto the brother of Jared, Behold, thou shalt make a hole in the top thereof, and also in the bottom thereof; and when thou shalt suffer for air, thou shalt unstop the hole thereof, and receive air. And if it so be that*

the water come in upon thee, behold, ye shall stop the hole
thereof, that ye may not perish in the flood.

—Ether 1:50–51 (2:20)

One can understand a hole in the top for fresh air, for access to the outside, and for collecting rainwater for drinking. Such a hole could then be quickly covered when a storm produced large waves. However, why make a hole in the bottom of a boat and risk sinking? What would be the purpose? If the top of that hole was above the waterline and a waterproof lid was available, there would have been no risk of sinking. The hole could then be used to get rid of wastes. Dropping a line down that hole with bait attached could provide a source of fresh fish to eat.

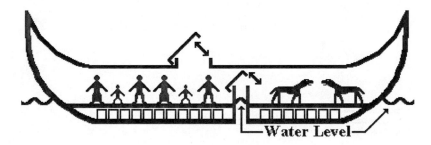

Sixteen Stones to Shine in Darkness

As the construction of the barges neared completion, the brother of Jared became concerned.

> *…O Lord, behold I have done even as thou hast com-*
> *manded me; and I have prepared the vessels for my people,*
> *and behold, there is no light in them. Behold, O Lord, wilt*
> *thou suffer that we shall cross this great water in darkness?*
> *And the Lord said unto the brother of Jared, What will*
> *ye that I should do that ye may have light in your vessels?*

—Ether 1:53–55 (2:22–23)

Windows were not allowed and they were not allowed to build a fire for light (Ether 1:56–59 [2:23–25]). However, to the Jaredites, a "window" would have had a different meaning. During that time, a window was a hole in the wall. A window may have been covered with shutters or a curtain to keep out the wind and rain. Glass windows were unknown until the time of the Romans many centuries later.

> And it came to pass that the brother of Jared…went forth unto the mount…Shelem…and did moulten out of a rock sixteen small stones and they were light and clear, even as transparent glass.
>
> —Ether 1:60–61 (3:1)

The brother of Jared spoke of this high mountain near where they camped by the sea (Ether 1:60 [3:1]). One possible mountain is the 5,000 foot Mount Tai on the Shandong Peninsula. It has been sacred to the Chinese for centuries.

Then the brother of Jared prayed:

> …touch these stones, O Lord, with thy finger, and prepare them that they may shine forth in darkness; and they shall shine forth unto us in the vessels which we have prepared, that we may have light while we cross the sea. Behold, O Lord, thou canst do this. We know that thou art able to shew forth great power, which looks small unto the understanding of men. And it came to pass that when the brother of Jared had said those words, behold, the Lord stretched forth his hand and touched the stones, one by one, with his finger…
>
> —Ether 1:66–68 (3:4–6)

...the brother of Jared came down out of the mount, and he did put forth the stones into the vessels which were pre-pared, one in each end thereof; and behold, they did give light unto the vessels thereof. And thus the Lord caused the stones to shine in darkness, to give light unto men, women and children, that they might not cross the great waters in darkness.

—Ether 3:1–2 (6:1–3)

How could a stone shine inside a darkened vessel? What was the nature of these stones? They were stones from the mountain that were melted and became transparent as glass. One suggested possibility is jade because it is sacred to both the Chinese and Olmec cultures. However, it has a very high melting point and is not clear as glass. Another suggestion is some kind of phosphorescent mineral. However, it needs an initial source of light energy which is stored and then released later as visible light for a few hours—not days! Again, it would not be clear as glass. A simple explanation is sandstone, quartzite, or quartz that was melted and then allowed to cool. It would easily form a stone that would be clear as glass.

A sturdy transparent material mounted into the wall or ceiling would have been a new concept to them. No familiar words could be used to describe it. When the Lord *"touched the stones,"* He must have also provided a new insight to the brother of Jared on the use of these stones.

One clear-as-glass stone mounted in the ceiling at each end of the eight vessels would be like a skylight. From inside the vessel, the stones would appear to shine in the darkness.

CROSSING THE GREAT SEA

And it came to pass that they had prepared all manner of food, that thereby they might subsist upon the water, and also food for their flocks and herds, and whatsoever beast, or animal, or fowl that they should carry with them.

—Ether 3:4 (6:4)

With final preparations made, they launched out into the deep.

And it came to pass that the Lord God caused that there should a furious wind blow upon the face of the waters, towards the promised land; and thus they were tossed upon the waves of the sea before the wind....they were many times buried in the depths of the sea, because of the mountain waves which broke upon them, and also the great and terrible tempests which were caused by the fierceness of the wind...when they were buried in the deep, there was no water that could hurt them, their vessels being tight like unto a dish…therefore when they were encompassed about by many waters, they did cry unto the Lord, and he did bring them forth again upon the top of the waters.

And thus they were driven forth, three hundred and forty and four days upon the water; and they did land upon the shore of the promised land.

—Ether 3:6–9, 13 (6:5–7, 11)

Being "*buried in the depths of the sea*" supports the absence of sails on these barges. Heavy seas could mean forty-foot waves washing over the top of their crafts, briefly burying them in the sea. For these people, unaccustomed to ocean storms, their descriptions may be understandably exaggerated.

An Atlantic Ocean crossing would have been shorter. However, the Jaredites' ocean journey took 344 days. This is evidence that they crossed the Pacific Ocean.

Even today, floating objects from Asia often reach the West Coast of the Americas after nearly a year of being adrift. A tsunami struck Japan in March 2011. In March 2012, "*a fishing vessel swept away by the Japanese tsunami…has been spotted off the coast of Canada.*"[8] More tsunami debris in the form of "*a 180-ton floating dock..washed ashore in Oregon in June 2012.*"[9]

---

8   "'Ghost ship' from Japan tsunami spotted off Canada." *Thejournal.ie.* 26 Mar 2012. <https://www.thejournal.ie/ghost-ship-from-japan-tsunami-spotted-off-canada-396272-Mar2012/> 3 Feb 2020.

9   Martin Fackler. "After the Tsunami, Japan's Sea Creatures Crossed an Ocean." *The New York Times.* 28 Sep 2017. <https://www.nytimes.com/2017/09/28/science/tsunami-japan-debris-ocean.html> 3 Feb 2020.

However, the Jaredite's journey covered a greater distance in less time than these examples. The Lord's help must have kept them in the middle of the current in addition to that *"furious wind."*

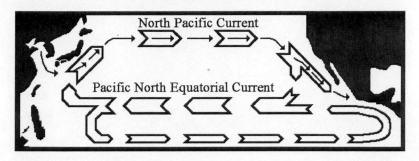

The North Pacific Current, about 45° N latitude, is a part of the North Pacific gyre, a huge coast-to-coast circular ocean current. In the summer, the days are much longer and the weather is warmer. This would have been more tolerable for those unaccustomed to a colder climate. Following this current could have easily brought the Jaredites to the western shore of Mexico.

Jaredite History in Mayan Legends

Fernando de Alva Cortés Ixtlilxóchitl was an indigenous native of Mexico at the time of the Spanish conquest. He wrote about the history of his people in the early seventeenth century. Hubert Howe Bancroft, in the late nineteenth century, frequently refers to his writings in his book on Mexico and Central American natives. According to Bancroft, Ixtlilxóchitl described a deluge during which

> *...man and all the earth were destroyed by great showers and by lightnings from heaven, so that nothing remained, and the most lofty mountains were covered up*

and submerged to the depth of caxtolmoleltli, or fifteen cubits...[10]

It is probably not a coincidence that the Bible describes Noah's flood as "*Fifteen cubits upward did the waters prevail; and the mountains were covered*" (Genesis 7:20, KJV). The Catholic missionaries certainly would have taught the Mayan natives about Noah. However, as we continue to read, the story takes on an additional twist. Ixtlilxóchitl describes a new generation of people who survived the deluge in some kind of chest (or ark?). Eventually, after generations had passed, they:

> *...built a zacuali of great height, and by this is meant a very high tower, in which to take refuge when the world should be a second time destroyed. After this their tongue became confused, and not understanding each other, they went to different parts of the world... The Toltecs, seven in number, with their wives, who understood each other's speech, after crossing great lands and seas, and finally arrived in America, which they found to be a good land, and fit for habitation...*[11]

In another part of his book, Bancroft again relates the same story from Ixtlilxóchitl.

> *...the building of a tower as a protection against a possible future* [flood], *and the confusion of tongues and consequent scattering of the population for all these things were found in the native traditions, as we are informed—seven*

---

10   Hubert H. Bancroft. *The Works of Hubert Howe Bancroft,* Vol. V, *The Native Races, Primitive History.* San Francisco, CA: A. L. Bancroft & Co., Publishers. 1883. p. 20.

11   Ibid. p. 21.

families speaking the same language kept together in their
wanderings for many years; and after crossing broad lands
and seas, enduring great hardships, they reached the coun-
try of Huehue Tlapallan or 'Old' Tlapallan, which they
found to be fertile and desirable to dwell in.[12]

It may be a coincidence that Ixtlilxóchitl described a group of people involved with a great tower and a confusion of tongues. As a convert to Christianity he would have been aware of these stories from the Bible. However, Ixtlilxóchitl went on to describe a close-knit family and friends, who spoke the same language after the confusion of tongues, and who crossed broad lands and seas to come to the Americas. This is a perfect description of the Jaredite journey!

A TRAIL OF CULTURAL CONNECTIONS

Reverence for a Leader's Name

In the ancient Egyptian culture, one would never call the pharaoh by name. That would suggest power over him, which was forbidden. One had to use a substitute name or symbol when referring to him. In some cases, it even extended to using a substitute name or symbol for the substitute. Similarly, in the Book of Ether, no other name was ever given for the brother of Jared.

The doctrine of the name is truly Babylonian....[It]
was an important part of their culture and they tried to
keep their names secret at certain times and on certain
occasions....This shows that the prime consequences of a
name is that its bearer becomes known and to this extent

---

12   Ibid. p. 209.

he becomes vulnerable…Since the knowledge of a person's name gave power over its owner, care was naturally taken to prevent it from becoming known.[13]

The Babylonian culture and Sumer were in the same geographic area and probably shared many cultural values.

If the Jaredites came from the Great Tower through Asia, the culture of reverence for the "older brother" appears to have followed them. In imperial China, the use of a ruler's given name was strictly taboo. "*In the Chinese culture, the elder brother is shown regard by using the respectful address 'elder brother,' rather than calling him by name.*"[14] He was often the spokesman or representative of the family. "*The eldest son… inherited the priestly duties of directing the family to God. It was his privilege to pray to or invoke God on behalf of others.*"[15]

In Chinese character writing, the Chinese pictograph for "mouth" or "speaking" is combined with the pictograph for "man" to create the ideograph meaning "eldest son." This ideograph for "eldest son" combined with the ideograph for "God" creates a new emblem meaning to "pray" or "invoke." All of this would seem to imply that whoever designed the original character symbology considered the eldest son to be the primary spokesman to God.[16]

Given these ancient traditions, it would be quite logical to assume that the brother of Jared was Jared's oldest brother. It appears that the

---

13   F. Edward Butterworth. *Pilgrims of the Pacific.* Independence, MO: Herald House, 1974. p. 23.

14   C. H. Kang and E. R. Nelson. *The Discovery of Genesis: How the Truths of Genesis Were Found in the Chinese Language.* St. Louis, MO: Concordia Publishing House, 1979. p. 85.

15   Ibid. p. 89.

16   Ibid. p. 89.

reverence given to the oldest son and respect for the name was already established and then passed along to their descendants.

The Chinese Characters and Genesis

The Jaredites departure from the Great Tower came at a time when they would have been familiar with the early events in the book of Genesis. Evidence suggests that whoever created the original Chinese characters must have been intimately familiar with those same stories.

Differing Chinese characters are combined to make new words. It is interesting that the symbols for "breath" (God breathing life into Adam) coupled with "two persons" (Adam and Eve) are included in the symbol for the word "garden."[17] The symbol for the word "flood" includes the symbol for the number "eight," suggesting that the original author was aware of the eight people on Noah's ark.[18] Except for the story of the confusion of tongues, it is difficult to understand why the symbol for the word "tower" includes the symbols for "mankind" and "mouth (speech)."[19] The authors Kang and Nelson even conjecture that the Chinese originally migrated from Mesopotamia at the time of the confusion of tongues.[20]

The Olmec and Chinese Characters

Mike Xu, a Texas Christian University professor, claimed to have proof, in the Olmec handwriting, that a group of Chinese immigrants may have sailed to the New World and changed the local culture there. This professor has spent years:

---

17   Ibid. p. 54

18   Ibid. p. 98

19   Ibid. p. 106

20   Ibid. p. 98

...analyzing jade, stone, and pottery relics from the Olmec....He was struck by how closely the symbols on the artifacts resembled Chinese inscriptions from the Shang Dynasty in China. "There are hundreds of these symbols that occur again and again, throughout the Olmec territory," Xu says....Olmec and Shang artistic styles look much alike, and the two cultures followed related religious practices. For instance, both used cinnabar, a red pigment, to decorate ceremonial objects, and both put jade beads in the mouths of the dead to ward off evil. "The similarities are just too striking to be a coincidence," he says.[21]

Mike Xu concluded that at the time of the fall of the Shang Dynasty (1122–1046 B.C.), some Chinese escaped by sea and ultimately found their way to Central America and founded the Olmec culture.[22] However, the Olmec culture had already been established centuries earlier.

When Jared, his brother, and their friends departed by sea, some of them may have remained behind. If these people had followed the Yellow River to the ocean, those who remained behind may have then established the beginnings of the Chinese culture. "*The Yellow River is..known as the 'cradle of Chinese civilization' or the 'Mother River.'*"[23] Those descendants of the Jaredites who remained behind may have become the founders of the ancient Xia Dynasty in China.

---

21   Jocelyn Selim. "Chinatown, 1000 B.C." *Discover.* Feb 2000. p. 20.

22   Ibid. p. 20.

23   Kallie Szczepanski. "The Yellow River's Role in China's History." *ThoughtCo.* 28 Jul 2019. <https://www.thoughtco.com/yellow-river-in-chinas-history-195222> 2 Jan 2020.

The Xia Dynasty, the earliest Chinese dynasty, is believed to have been established around 2070 B.C.[24] This timeframe fits the estimated arrival of the brother of Jared and his people. When the Xia Dynasty was defeated, some elements of their culture quite likely continued as part of the succeeding Shang Dynasty.

Physical Traits of the Olmec and Chinese

Olmec Collossal Stone Head

Another interesting trait that connects the Olmec with the Asian Culture is the epicanthic eye fold that is common in Asia and depictions seen on the Olmec colossal stone heads. Some have suggested that the broad noses on the Olmec stone heads are evidence of African descent. However, the Jaredites departed from the Middle East where a wide nose would not have been uncommon. *"The southern Chinese...are characteri[ze]ed by a long head, a short face, a low and wide nose, and low eyes."*[25] The suggestion that the Olmec and the southern Chinese cultures shared a common ancestor now becomes more plausible.

24   "Xia Dynasty—Ancient China's First Dynasty." *China Highlights.* < https:// www.chinahighlights.com/travelguide/china-history/the-xia-dynasty.htm > 20 Nov 2019.

25   X. J. Wu, W. Liu, and C. J. Bae. "Craniofacial Variation Between Southern and Northern Neolithic and Modern Chinese." *International Journal of Osteoarchaeology,* Vol. 22. Wiley Online Library. 22 Jul 2010. p. 102. <https:// pdfs.semanticscholar.org/1dbe/d653578fc458dc291af872725d323db0bb1c. pdf> 15 Nov 2019.

CONCLUSION

In light of the evidence from the Book of Mormon and Chinese cultural connections, the Jaredites likely gave rise to both the Olmec culture of Central Mexico and the early Xia Dynasty of China by those who were left behind.

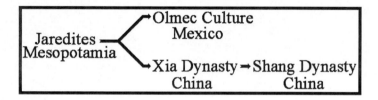

Stories from the Bible and Book of Mormon combined with geography, oceanography, and the histories and legends of early cultures provide one compatible story. All of this complements and supports the description of the Jaredite journey as described in the Book of Mormon. I believe the Jaredites were...

REAL PEOPLE IN REAL PLACES!

CHAPTER 2

JAREDITE FLESH
ON OLMEC SKELETONS

I was astonished a couple of years ago when I attended a Mayan Archaeology conference. A speaker was showing maps representing the distribution of the Olmec civilization in Mexico. The first map indicated a large area representing the Olmec heartland. The next map represented the distribution of the Olmec sometime later in their history. What struck me immediately was that the second map showed the outer edges of the Olmec population had remained essentially the same. However, the population in the center of the original territory was gone—simply vanished from history! The final battle of the Jaredites immediately came to mind. The era of the Jaredites, as described in the Book of Mormon, ended with warring factions that resulted in the deaths of millions of people.

Overcome by curiosity, I felt led to do an in-depth study of Olmec archaeology and history and compare that with the history of the Jaredites found in the Book of Mormon. I started by focusing on the final battles. However, as I explored the Olmec history, I found several occasions in which there was an apparent social upheaval and shifting populations. While comparing what is known of Olmec history, I found some fascinating geographical and archaeological correlations with Jaredite history.

Any attempt to correlate the Olmec and Jaredite histories has its challenges. The Olmec names have long since disappeared from history. The finite histories of both are sketchy, at best.

The history of the Jaredites was a history of varying leaders. Some were righteous. Some were self-centered, seeking gain, control over a particular population, or revenge for a perceived offense. There were times of peace and multiple times of war. The descriptions give only a few hints regarding geography.

This chapter is an attempt to provide an overview of Moroni's summary of the history of the Jaredites correlated with the ancient Olmec culture. Estimates among Book of Mormon scholars have placed the arrival time of the Jaredites at somewhere between 2100 and 2000 B.C. Archaeologists suggest that the Olmec culture was established sometime before 1600 B.C. Any new group of people would not leave an immediate archaeological footprint that documents the time of their arrival. This would be especially true with a small group and would explain such a discrepancy.

The Arrival of the Jaredites in the Americas

It is assumed that the Jaredites landed on the Pacific coast of Mexico near the Isthmus of Tehuantepec. Accustomed to years of migrating across Asia, the Jaredites must have resumed their migratory lifestyle after their arrival. They would have had a natural desire to explore this new land. There is a narrow pass, the Chivela Pass, leading across southern Mexico to the Gulf of Mexico—a distance of about 125 miles. The Olmec Heartland is centered along the Gulf Coast side of the Isthmus. As they explored, they would have discovered many resources for a growing community.

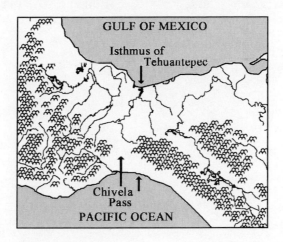

Rapid Growth of Population

The Book of Ether indicates a tendency to have large families.

And Jared had four sons…And the brother of Jared also begat sons and daughters. And the friends of Jared and his brother, were in number about twenty and two souls; and they also begat sons and daughters, before they came to the promised land; and therefore they began to be many… Now the number of the sons and daughters of the brother of Jared were twenty and two souls; and the number of the sons and daughters of Jared were twelve, he having four sons.

—Ether 3:16–18, 22–23 (6:14–16, 20)

If having such large families were normal, it would take only a few generations for the population to easily exceed 1,000. As populations grew, groups would separate into more distant regions. More distant colonies would have developed slightly different cultures due to different resources and environmental issues. Trade between population centers would have provided not only a stabilizing force creating a basis for unity but also a potential for rivalry and warfare.

San Lorenzo and La Venta

Evidence will be developed within this chapter to suggest that the two main cities occupied by the Jaredites have their equivalent with the two main cities occupied by the Olmec. They were La Venta and San Lorenzo.

The Jaredite population would have settled first in the area known as San Lorenzo Tenochtitlan. At that time, it was a large island in the Coatzacoalcos River. This became known among the Jaredites as the land of Nehor. However, the land of Nehor or the city of Nehor is only mentioned twice in the early part of the history of the Jaredites (Ether 3:41, 46 [7:4, 9]). It became known later as the land of their first inheritance. Both are understood to be a reference to the Olmec site of San Lorenzo.

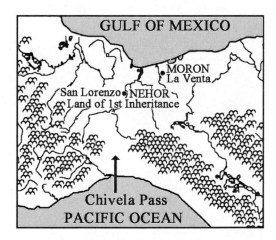

The other major site is La Venta, located near the Tonalá River. Closer to the seashore meant the availability of seafood. This site became known among the Jaredites as the land of Moron after one of the later rulers, King Moron.

For both San Lorenzo and La Venta, the associated rivers would have provided a steady source of water for drinking and irrigation. Both sites are on elevated ground—avoiding problems with occasional flooding. The higher ground would also provide a military advantage during times of war.

BEFORE ARCHAEOLOGICAL RECORD

There is very little in the way of an archaeological record during the early time frame. However, many of the archaeological correlations illustrated later in the chapter have their foundations here.

The Brother of Jared

After his arrival in this new world,

> ...*the brother of Jared began to be old, and saw that he must soon go down to the grave; wherefore he saith unto Jared, Let us gather together our people, that we may number them, that we may know of them what they will desire of us before we go down to our graves.*
>
> —Ether 3:21 (6:19)

The people decided they wanted a king. "*But the brother of Jared said unto them, Surely, this thing leadeth into captivity*" (Ether 3:27 [6:23]). Nevertheless, the youngest son of Jared reluctantly agreed to be their king.

Brother of Jared's Prophecy Fulfilled

Jared's great-grandson, Corihor:

> *...rebelled against his father* [in Moron/La Venta]... *and dwelt in the land of Nehor* [San Lorenzo]... *Corihor drew away many people after him...gathered together an army...took* [his father] *captive, which brought to pass the saying of the brother of Jared, That they would be brought into captivity.*
>
> —Ether 3:41–42 (7:4–5)

Corihor brought his father and his people to live in Nehor as his servants. As servants, they would endure minimal living conditions while continuing to have children. Corihor's father had another son, Shule, while in captivity (Ether 3:44 [7:7]). Shule grew up in the Land of Nehor. When he was older, he

> *...was angry with his brother...waxed strong, and became mighty, as to the strength of a man...Wherefore he came to the hill Ephraim, and he did moulten out of the hill, and made swords out of steel for those which he had drew away with him; and...he had armed them with swords...*
>
> —Ether 3:45–46 (7:8–9)

In the mountainous valley, ESE of San Lorenzo, are deposits of magnetite (iron oxide) and ilmenite (iron/titanium oxide). The hill Ephraim may have been in this area. This resource was sufficiently abundant such that in later years, the city of Chiapa de Corzo would be established. A trade relationship involving magnetite and ilmenite would develop between Chiapa de Corzo and San Lorenzo.[26]

> [Shule] *returned to the city Nehor, and gave battle unto his brother Corihor, by which means he obtained the kingdom, and restored it unto his father Kib. And now because of the thing which Shule had done, his father bestowed upon him the kingdom; therefore he began to reign in the stead of his father.*
>
> —Ether 3:46–47 (7:9–10)

---

26 Timothy D. Sullivan, graduate thesis. "The Social and Political Evolution of Chiapa de Corzo, Chiapas, Mexico: An Analysis of Changing Strategies of Rulership in a Middle Formative Through Early Classic Mesoamerican Political Center" University of Pittsburgh, 2009. pp. 71–72. <https://www.researchgate.net/publication/292984759> 12 Dec 2017.

More Rebellion and a Divided Kingdom

It appears that King Shule remained in the Land of Nehor where he had lived his entire life rather than moving back to where his father had once ruled. Nevertheless, he was now king over the entire kingdom. His brother, Corihor, repented of his vengeful ways. As a result, King Shule gave Corihor power over his kingdom (Land of Nehor/San Lorenzo). However, Shule was still king over the whole kingdom—including the Land of Nehor and the Land of Moron.

Corihor had two sons, Noah and Cohor. During their youth, these two sons were probably exposed to the animosity between their father, and his brother, King Shule. They probably also recalled those days when their father reigned over the whole kingdom. Just as Corihor had rebelled against his father, Corihor's sons rebelled against him.

These two sons, along with many others, went into battle against their father and King Shule. Noah "*carried* [King Shule] *away captive into Moron*" (Ether 3:55 [7:17]). Carrying him away captive into Moron suggests that Noah intended to rule over the whole kingdom including both the land of Nehor and the land of Moron. His revenge was to force Shule and his people to become his servants.

Shule was subsequently rescued by his sons. In the process, Noah was killed. Shule returned to his kingdom—the land of their first inheritance/land of Nehor (San Lorenzo).

From that point on, the Jaredite kingdom "*was divided; and there was two kingdoms, the kingdom of Shule, and the kingdom of Cohor, the son of Noah*" (Ether 3:58 [7:20]).

Location of the Wilderness of Akish

One particular person of interest in the succeeding sequence of rulers was King Akish who lived in the land of their first inheritance (San Lorenzo). He was so cruel, his sons turned against him. Later battles appear to have been fought in the "wilderness of Akish"—probably an isolated forest near San Lorenzo.

ARCHAEOLOGICAL CONNECTIONS

While searching the histories of the Olmec and Jaredites, I began to find significant correlations. The evidence from archaeological history provided approximate dates. The sequence of events given in the Book of Ether provided an explanation for the cause of perplexing incidents in archaeological history.

King Heth—1600 B.C.

There is an Olmec archaeological site known as El Manati, about nine miles southeast of San Lorenzo.

> *El Manati was the site of a sacred Olmec sacrificial bog from roughly 1600 BCE until 1200 BCE, it is likely that this site…was used for ritual ceremonies which included offerings…all found in an excellent state of preservation in the muck.*[27]
>
> *…at the El Manati site, disarticulated skulls and femurs as well as complete skeletons of newborn or unborn children have been discovered amidst the other offerings,*

---

27 "El Manati." *WikiVisually.* <https://wikivisually.com/wiki/El_Manat%C3%AD> 21 Nov 2019.

leading to speculation concerning infant sacrifice. It is not yet known, though, how the infants met their deaths.[28]

El Manati appears to have been more of a shrine and the location of what is believed by some to have been a sacrificial bog. Infant sacrifice has been suggested; however, it may have simply been the result of high infant mortality.

The time associated with El Manati may have included the reign of King Heth in the land of their first inheritance (San Lorenzo). He was a wicked king who had killed his father to gain the throne. Warnings came from prophets of the Lord to repent or there would be a curse on the land. Those prophets were cast out or "*cast into pits,* [muddy bogs of El Manati?] *and left to perish*" (Ether 4:33 [9:29]).

> *And it came to pass that there began to be a great dearth upon the land, and the inhabitants began to be destroyed exceeding fast…for there was no rain upon the face of the earth; and there came forth poisonous serpents also upon the face of the land, and did poison many people.*
>
> —Ether 4:35 (9:30–31)

---

28 "Olmec Civilization." *Crystallinks.com.* <https://www.crystalinks.com/olmec. html> 21 Nov 2019.

The poisonous serpent was probably the fer-de-lance, the ultimate pit viper. It is very aggressive and very fast. It ranges from Central Mexico to northern South America. It is mainly terrestrial and nocturnal. A severe drought would have dropped the water levels allowing this terrestrial snake to have easy access to what was then the island of San Lorenzo. An adult fer-de-lance may range from four to more than eight feet long. The preferred prey includes small animals found around tropical homes. The fer-de-lance is often the leading cause of snakebite poisoning within its range.[29] The venom causes tissue death which may result in the loss of a limb—if the victim survives. The venom can also cause widespread internal bleeding. The result would have been a high mortality rate—especially among infants and small children.

Coatzacoalcos is the name of the river associated with San Lorenzo. It is interesting that "*Coatzacoalcos comes from a Nahuatl word meaning 'Site of the Snake' or 'Where the snake hides'*"[30]

We are told in the Book of Ether that many animals fled from the poisonous serpents and that King Heth died as a result of the famine. Eventually, the rains returned, the drought was over, and the kingdom recovered under the leadership of a descendant of Heth.

For a time, those poisonous serpents would continue to breed on the island.

---

29   "Central American Fer-De-Lance, Bothrops asper." *The Dallas World Aquarium.* <https://dwazoo.com/animal/central-american-fer-de-lance/> 21 Nov 2019.

30   "Coatzacoalcos" *Wikipedia, the Free Encyclopedia.* <https://en.wikipedia.org/wiki/Coatzacoalcos> 8 Jul 2019.

Although established for several centuries, San Lorenzo:

> *had its heyday between 1200–900 BC. Temples, plazas, roadways and kingly residences are included in an area of about a half-acre, where about 1,000 people resided."*[31]

> *Starting in 1200 B.C. in the steamy jungles of Mexico's southern Gulf Coast, the Olmec's influence spread as far as modern Guatemala, Honduras, Belize, Costa Rica, and El Salvador. They built large settlements, established elaborate trade routes and developed religious iconography and rituals…*[32]

The timing may coincide with the reign of King Lib. In the days of Lib, the people *"built a great city by the narrow neck of land…."* (Ether 4:68 [10:20]).

"And in the days of Lib the poisonous serpents were destroyed…" (Ether 4:66 [10:19]). With the return of normal water levels and a concerted effort by the people over multiple generations, these terrestrial poisonous serpents could have been eliminated on the island of San Lorenzo.

> *And they did preserve the land southward for a wilderness, to get game. And the whole face of the land northward was covered with inhabitants; and they were exceeding*

---

31 K. Kris Hirst. "San Lorenzo (Mexico)" *Thought Co.* 7 Mar 2017. <https://www.thoughtco.com/san-lorenzo-mexico-olmec-172604> 16 Sep 2019.

32 Michael D. Lemonick. "Mystery of the Olmec." *Time.* 24 Jun 2001. <http://content.time.com/time/magazine/article/0,9171,136151,00.html> 24 Oct 2019.

industrious, and they did buy and sell, and traffic one with another, that they might get gain.

—Ether 4:69–70 (10:21–22)

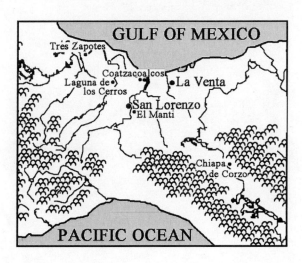

The land southward from the land of their first inheritance (San Lorenzo) would be toward the Pacific Ocean side of the Isthmus of Tehuantepec. Notice that there is a lack of major Olmec sites to the south of San Lorenzo. The land northward from San Lorenzo has been called the Olmec Heartland because of the numerous Olmec sites. Only thirty-three miles from the Gulf of Mexico, San Lorenzo could easily control commerce along the Coatzacoalcos River.

King Com—900 B.C.

Around 900 BCE the site of San Lorenzo displays evidence of systematic destruction whilst La Venta, conversely, began to flourish, and becoming the new capital, it eventually supported a population of some 18,000.[33]

33   Mark Cartwright. "Olmec Civilization." *Ancient History Encyclopedia*. 4 Apr 2018. <https://www.ancient.eu/Olmec_Civilization/> 24 Sep 2018.

On this map, the sites marked with a circle were seriously diminished or abandoned by 900 B.C. La Venta, about fifty miles northeast of San Lorenzo grew in size. Two Olmec sites known as Tres Zapotes and Chiapa de Corzo were far enough away such that they did not seem to have been negatively affected by the same pressures.

The reasons for this apparent migration away from San Lorenzo have been debated. This shift in population might have been associated with the reign of King Com.

> *...Com drew away the half of the kingdom. And he reigned over the half of the kingdom* [La Venta] *forty and two years; and he went to battle against the king Amgid* [San Lorenzo], *and they fought for the space of many years, in the which Com gained power over Amgid and obtained power over the remainder of the kingdom.*
>
> —Ether 4:86–87 (10:32)

After defeating King Amgid, the power authority in the kingdom resided entirely in the land of Moron (La Venta).

King Moron—600 B.C.

> [San Lorenzo] *was abandoned for some years before...*
> [600 B.C.]. *These later inhabitants* [after 600 B.C.] *con-*
> *tributed some small mounds and a ball court. The site was*
> *then abandoned for over a thousand years...*[34]

This meager recolonization effort is likely to have been the result of a competition or confrontation between the kingdoms of San Lorenzo and La Venta.

A descendant of Com by the name of Moron came to power. King Moron reigned over the land of Moron (La Venta).

> *...and Moron did do that which was wicked before the*
> *Lord. And it came to pass that there arose a rebellion*
> *among the people, because of that secret combination*
> *which was built up to get power and gain; and there arose*
> *a mighty man among them and gave battle unto Moron,*
> *in the which he did overthrow the half of the kingdom; and*
> *he did maintain the half of the kingdom* [San Lorenzo]
> *for many years.*
>
> —Ether 4:106–107 (11:14–15)

Eventually, Moron regained the entire kingdom by overthrowing this unknown pretender to his throne.

---

34   Christopher Minster. "The Historic Olmec City of San Lorenzo" *ThoughtCo.* 15 Jun 2019. <https://www.thoughtco.com/the-olmec-city-of-san-lorenzo-2136302> 23 Nov 2019.

And it came to pass that there arose another mighty man;
and…he did overthrow Moron and obtain the kingdom;
wherefore Moron dwelt in captivity all the remainder of
his days…

—Ether 4:109–110 (11:17–18)

After the defeat of Moron, the land of their first inheritance (San Lorenzo) was again in control. Moron's son also lived in captivity all his days. This period may represent that brief recolonizing effort of San Lorenzo.

Mulekite First Landing—586–585 B.C.

The Mulekites, who will be discussed in Chapter 4, arrived from across the Atlantic Ocean around 586–585 B.C. Upon their arrival, the Mulekites may have briefly come ashore, the land of Desolation[35] *"being the place of their first landing"* (Alma 13:74 [22:30]). Perhaps sensing some ongoing hostilities or simply finding a large population that spoke a very foreign language, they departed. The Mulekites eventually settled further south on the Yucatan Peninsula.

King Coriantumr—400 B.C.

According to the archaeological evidence, that brief influence of San Lorenzo that began in 600 B.C. ended about 400 B.C. During those years, there must have been a continuing struggle for domination over the whole kingdom. Ether, who wrote the summary of the history of the Jaredites, was a witness of the events during the time of King

---

35   The land of Desolation is a reference to the area around La Venta. The name would be given to this area by the Nephites many years later.

Coriantumr. Coriantumr had become *"king over all the land"* (Ether 5:1 [12:1]) and his throne was in the land of Moron (La Venta).

Ether was a prophet of the Lord and tried in vain to warn Coriantumr to repent.

> *...but they esteemed him as nought, and cast him out, and he hid himself in the cavity of a rock by day, and by night he went forth viewing the things which should come upon the people. And as he dwelt in the cavity of a rock, he made the remainder of this record, viewing the destructions which came upon the people by night.*
>
> —Ether 6:14–15 (13:13–14)

Ether returned later to deliver a prophecy to Coriantumr.

> *...the word of the Lord came to Ether, that he should go and prophesy unto Coriantumr, that if he would repent, and all his household, the Lord would give unto him his kingdom, and spare the people, otherwise they should be destroyed...save it were himself...and he should only live to see the fulfilling of the prophecies...concerning another people receiving the land for their inheritance and Coriantumr should receive a burial by them; and every soul should be destroyed save it were Coriantumr...*
>
> —Ether 6:21–23 (13:20–21)

Coriantumr sought to kill Ether but he fled again to hide *"in the cavity of a rock"* (Ether 6:24 [13:22]). This was most likely a cave.

Three years later, Coriantumr was defeated in battle by Shared and he lived as a captive. During the following year, the sons of

Coriantumr gained his release. Coriantumr then built up an army to fight Shared.

> *And it came to pass that Coriantumr…went against [Shared] with his armies, to battle…and they did meet in the valley of Gilgal…And it came to pass that Shared fought against him for the space of three days. And it came to pass that Coriantumr…did pursue him until he came to the plains of Heshlon. And it came to pass that Shared…did beat Coriantumr, and drove him back again to the valley of Gilgal…Coriantumr gave Shared battle again in the valley of Gilgal, in the which he beat Shared, and slew him.*
>
> —Ether 6:29–33 (14:27–30)

A valley large enough to host two large battling armies would suggest a mountainous valley. The closest large valley might have been a valley in the Tuxtla Mountains, located about sixty miles from La Venta. Alternating elevations and tropical forests in the area would have provided advantages and challenges for both armies. If the Valley of Gilgal was associated with the Tuxtla Mountains, the Plains of Heshlon may have been located between La Venta and the Tuxtla Mountains.

In the end, Coriantumr killed Shared but was wounded in the process. Coriantumr probably returned to his home (Land of Moron/La Venta) where he could feel safe during his recovery.

Two years later, the brother of Shared went into battle against Coriantumr.

> *And it came to pass that the brother of Shared did give battle unto him in the wilderness of Akish; and the battle*

became exceeding sore, and many thousands fell by the sw014 And it came to pass that Coriantumr did lay siege to the wilderness, and the brother of Shared did march forth out of the wilderness by night, and slew a part of the army of Coriantumr, as they were drunken.

—Ether 6:38–39 (14:4–5)

As mentioned before, the wilderness of Akish was probably near the land of their first inheritance (San Lorenzo). The idea that Coriantumr could lay siege to the wilderness of Akish suggests that it was an isolated forested area.

After the brother of Shared defeated Coriantumr's army, he "*came forth to the land of Moron, and placed himself upon the throne of Coriantumr*" (Ether 6:10 [14:6]). Shared was making an obvious attempt to declare himself to be the king over the whole land. This is also evidence that Coriantumr's throne/center of political power was in the land of Moron (La Venta). It was now lost to Coriantumr and he wanted his throne back!

While Coriantumr hid out to build up his army, the Brother of Shared was killed and a new leader, Lib, came to power. This Lib may have been named after that Lib that built that "*great city.*"

…in the first year of Lib, Coriantumr came up unto the land of Moron, and gave battle unto Lib…he fought with Lib, in the which Lib did smite upon his arm, that he was wounded; nevertheless, the army of Coriantumr did press forward upon Lib, that he fled to the borders upon the seashore.

—Ether 6:45–46 (14:11–12)

During the battle by the seashore, Lib defeated the army of Corantumr, who then fled to the wilderness of Akish.

> *And it came to pass that Lib did pursue him until he came to the plains of Agosh. And Coriantumr had taken all the people with him, as he fled...*
>
> —Ether 6:49–50 (14:15).

The plains of Agosh were probably open fields such as a floodplain. If the wilderness of Akish was near San Lorenzo, then the plains of Agosh might have been somewhere between the land of Moron (La Venta) and the land of their first inheritance (San Lorenzo).

Coriantumr met Lib in battle and Lib was killed. Coriantumr probably celebrated regaining his lost throne!

More on the Location of the Land of Moron

There is an interesting reference to the land of Moron that helps to validate the location.

"Now the land of Moron where the king dwelt, was near the land which is called Desolation by the Nephites" (Ether 3:43 [7:6]). Many years later, the area would be called the land of Desolation by the Nephites after they discovered the carnage from the final battles among the Jaredites. It was also written many years later regarding the Nephite, Hagoth.

> *And it came to pass that Hagoth, he being an exceed-ing curious man, therefore he went forth and built him an exceeding large ship, on the borders of the land Bountiful, by the land Desolation, and launched it forth*

into the West Sea, by the narrow neck which led into the land northward.

—Alma 30:6 (63:5)

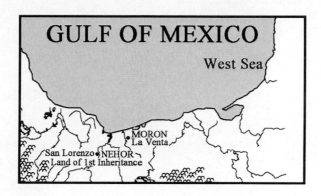

From these sources, it would appear that the land of Moron was near the land Desolation, the West Sea, and the narrow neck (Isthmus of Tehuantepec). This reference to the West Sea likely refers to the western side of the Yucatan Peninsula where many of the Nephites lived. When taken together, this supports the idea that the land of Moron refers to La Venta.

King Coriantumr — Final Battles

After the death of Lib, his brother, Shiz, took his place and the war continued!

> *And it came to pass that Shiz pursued after Coriantumr, and he did overthrow many cities, and he did slay both women and children, and he did burn the cities thereof; and there went a fear of Shiz throughout all the land; yea, a cry went forth throughout the land: Who can stand before the army of Shiz? Behold, he sweepeth the earth before him!*

—Ether 6:53–54 (14:17–18)

La Venta/Land of Moron/center of Coriantumr's kingdom would have been an obvious target for Shiz. Archaeologists have seen evidence of intentional destruction of some of the buildings and monuments in La Venta. A carbon sample from a burned area found on the surface of the "Great Pyramid" of La Venta resulted in a carbon date of 394 +/– 30 B.C.[36] This precisely fits the time frame described in the Book of Mormon.

> *And it came to pass that the people began to flock together in armies, throughout all the face of the land…a part of them fled to the army of Shiz, and a part of them fled to the army of Coriantumr.—And so great and lasting had been the war, and so long had been the scene of bloodshed and carnage, that the whole face of the land was covered with the bodies of the dead…there was none left to bury the dead, but they did march forth from the shedding of blood, to the shedding of blood, leaving the bodies of both men, women and children, strewed upon the face of the land, to become a prey to the worms of the flesh.*
>
> —Ether 6:55–58 (14:19–22)

The ensuing battles appear to have covered a large territory.

> *Now the loss of men, women and children, on both sides, were so great that Shiz commanded his people that they should not pursue the armies of Coriantumr; wherefore*

---

36   Arlene Coleman. Graduate thesis. "The Construction of Complex A at La Venta, Tabasco, Mexico: A History of Buildings, Burials, Offerings, and Stone Monuments." Provo, Utah: Brigham Young University. Aug 2010. p. 53. <https://www.academia.edu/11950743/The_Construction_of_Complex_A_at_La_Venta_Tabasco_Mexico_A_History_of_Building_Burials_Offerings_and_Stone_Monuments> 16 Aug 2019.

they returned to their camp…when Coriantumr had recovered of his wounds, he began to remember the words which Ether had spoken unto him: He saw that there had been slain by the sword already nearly two millions of his people, and he began to sorrow in his heart; yea, there had been slain two millions of mighty men, and also their wives and their children.

—Ether 6:71–73 (14:31–15:2)

If Coriantumr had lost two million of his mighty men, and if the two sides had been equally matched, then Shiz also lost two million of his mighty men. Add to that number, their wives and children. Also, consider that the war was not yet over! It is this thought that came to mind when I remembered those two maps mentioned at the beginning of this chapter. I recalled that huge hole in that second map representing the vanished Olmec population.

Coriantumr sent a message to Shiz pleading for peace but it was rejected.

And it came to pass that he [Coriantumr] came to the waters of Ripliancum, which, by interpretation, is large, or to exceed all; wherefore, when they came to these waters, they pitched their tents; and Shiz also pitched his tents, near unto them; and therefore, on the morrow, they did come to battle.

—Ether 6:80 (15:8)

Coriantumr was wounded but his army caused the army of Shiz to flee.

When Moroni wrote about the waters of Ripliancum, he felt it necessary to define the term. It may have been a Jaredite / Sumerian term unfamiliar to any potential Jewish reader. One author explored the possible root words found in "Ripliancum." He suggested the following: rib (surpassing); la (flooding); ana (as much as); ku-um (to spread).[37] All of this suggests a large body of water.

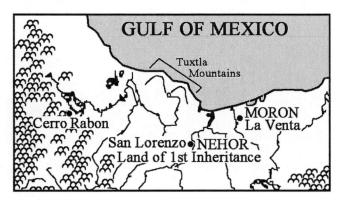

In the middle of the Tuxtla Mountains, Laguna Catemaco is the largest lake in what is considered to be the Olmec heartland. Ripliancum may have been this twenty-eight-square-mile freshwater lake.

The army of Shiz then traveled southwesterly to a place called Ogath. Moroni wrote:

> *And it came to pass that the army of Coriantumr did pitch their tents by the hill Ramah; and it was the same hill where my father Mormon did hide up the records unto the Lord, which were sacred.*
>
> —Ether 6:83 (15:11)

---

37   Jerry D. Grover. *Sumerian Roots of Jaredite-Derived Names and Terminology in the Book of Mormon.* Provo, UT: Challex Scientific Publications. 2017. p. 39.

Some believe that this Hill Ramah, called Hill Cumorah by the Nephites, is Cerro Rabon.[38] It is also located southwest of Laguna Catemaco.

For the next four years, Coriantumr and Shiz proceeded to gather together all the people in the land. Time and resources were also needed to produce more armament and weapons.

Then after four years and another unsuccessful plea for peace, the two armies fought.

> *And it came to pass that when they had all fallen by the sword, save it were Coriantumr and Shiz, behold, Shiz had fainted with loss of blood. And it came to pass that when Coriantumr had leaned upon his sword, that he rested a little, he smote off the head of Shiz.*
>
> —Ether 6:103–104 (15:29–30)

Ether survived as a silent witness and left a record of the things he had seen.

The Olmec culture came to an end around 400 B.C.

Coriantumr's Final Days

"..*Coriantumr was discovered by the people of Zarahemla* [Mulekites]*; and he dwelt with them for the space of nine Moons*" (Omni 1:37 [1:21]). It is noteworthy that this memory of Coriantumr among the Mulekites, in the chronology of the Book of Mormon, was written before Ether's record ever came to light.

---

38   There is further clarification in Chapter 9 regarding Cerro Rabon/Hill Cumorah/Hill Ramah.

SOME OLMEC / JAREDITES SURVIVE

Recall that during the days of Lib (1200 B.C), the Jaredite/Olmec culture had spread far beyond the borders of the Olmec heartland. The Mulekites had probably developed an ongoing trade relationship with other Jaredite/Olmec colonies while trying to avoid political entanglements. This might explain how some of the Mulekites would have been able to remember and probably converse with Coriantumr during his final days.

Ether wrote of those warring factions. He described how they had gathered all the people into their respective armies and all had been killed. However, Ether could only be referring to those people in the areas where he was a witness. More distant areas could have easily survived. This would include at least two noteworthy Olmec sites. They were Tres Zapotes and Chiapa de Corzo, at opposite ends of the Olmec heartland.

> *Between 1000 and 400 B.C. ... Tres Zapotes was a minor regional center covering around 200 acres...Around 400 B.C., La Venta abruptly collapsed...Researchers believe that it's possible many of them moved to Tres Zapotes, 60 miles to the west. The city quickly expanded, covering 1,200 acres by... [or] shortly after 400 B.C.*[39]

Refugees who did not want to participate in these battles were trying to escape. At the same time, Tres Zapotes adopted a different style of leadership—as though a shared form of government as opposed to a single king.[40] Each group must have been peacefully accommo-

---

39   Grover. pp. 27-28.
40   Ibid. pp. 28-29.

dated. As a result, the Olmec culture would survive in Tres Zapotes for several more centuries.

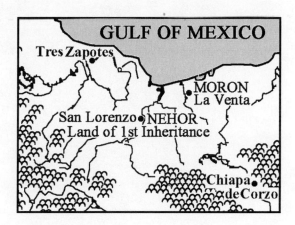

On the other end of the Olmec Heartland is Chiapa de Corzo. It appears to have been initially connected with the Olmec. As it borders between the Olmec and the early Mayan regions (Mulekites), it could easily have been a trading post between two very different cultures.

Archaeologically, Chiapa de Corzo shows evidence of Olmec occupation during the Early and Middle Preclassic periods [2000–400 B.C.] *and Maya occupation during the Late Preclassic* [beginning in 400 B.C.]…[41]

As the Olmec culture declined, the Mayan influence in Chiapa de Corzo became dominant.

---

41   Loa P. Traxler and Robert J. Sharer, ed. *The Origins of Maya States*. Philadelphia, University of Pennsylvania Press: 2016. p. 165.

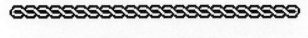

CONCLUSION

The similarities and coincidences of two very sketchy histories between the Olmec and the Jaredites are hard to deny. It is Jaredite flesh on an archaeologically bare Olmec skeleton that allows us to appreciate a bigger story. I believe these Jaredites were…

REAL PEOPLE IN REAL PLACES!

CHAPTER 3:

LEHI'S ROUTE TO THE PROMISED LAND

Introduction

The Book of Mormon begins with the words of Lehi's son, Nephi. He described the journey of his father and traveling companions from Jerusalem to the Promised Land. As a first-hand account, more details are provided on their journey than for either the Jaredites or the Mulekites.

LEHI'S EARLY YEARS

During the time that Josiah was the king of Judah, he ordered the Temple to be repaired. In the process of repairing the Temple, an interesting discovery was made.

> *And it came to pass in the eighteenth year of king Josiah [c. 622 B.C.], that the king sent Shaphan…to the house of the Lord….And Hilkiah the high priest said unto Shaphan the scribe, I have found the book of the law in the house of the Lord. And Hilkiah gave the book to Shaphan, and he read it. And Shaphan the scribe came to the king… And Shaphan the scribe shewed the king, saying, Hilkiah the priest hath delivered me a book. And Shaphan read it before the king.*
>
> —2 Kings 22:3, 8–10, KJV

What followed was sincere repentance on the part of Josiah and the beginning of Josiah's reform. Pagan altars and idols were removed from the Temple. Pagan worship and fertility cults were banned. The worship of YHWH became centralized in the Temple. Passover was celebrated with huge feasts.

Lehi had to have been an eyewitness to all of these changing events and familiar with the renewed focus on worshipping YHWH. The reforms of King Josiah must have had a positive influence on Lehi's outlook on life. It is noteworthy that Lehi's four sons were probably in their teenage years during this time.

About thirteen years after the beginning of this reform, King Josiah (609 B.C.) died. His son, Jehoahaz, became king. However, he was king for only about three months before being taken to Egypt where Pharaoh Necho II had him imprisoned.

Pharaoh Necho appointed Jehoahaz's older brother, Jehoiakim, to be the king of Judah.

> *Rabbinical literature describes Jehoiakim as a godless tyrant who committed atrocious sins and crimes. He is portrayed as living in incestuous relations with his mother, daughter-in-law, and stepmother, and was in the habit of murdering men, whose wives he then violated and whose property he seized. He also had tattooed his body.*[42]

Jehoiakim owed his allegiance and paid tribute to Egypt. However, in 605 B.C., King Nebuchadnezzar of Babylon defeated Egypt. Jehoiakim then altered his allegiance and paid tribute to

---

42   Emil G. Hirsch, et al. "Jehoiakim." *Jewish Encyclopedia.* 1906. <http://www.jewishencyclopedia.com/articles/8562-jehoiakim> 28 Dec 2019.

Nebuchadnezzar. In 601 B.C., Nebuchadnezzar went to battle against Egypt for a second time. This time there was no decisive winner. This may be when Jehoiakim switched his allegiance back to Egypt. As a result, King Nebuchadnezzar laid siege to Jerusalem (598 B.C.).

Lehi's sons came of age during the time of Jehoiakim. The self-centered power-hungry idol-worshipping regime of Jehoiakim probably influenced Lehi's older rebellious sons, Laman and Lemuel.

During the siege by Nebuchadnezzar, Jehoiakim died and was replaced by his son, Jehoiachin. Jerusalem fell to Nebuchadnezzar three months later.

Nebuchadnezzar designated Jehoiakim's uncle, Zedekiah, king. It was during "*the commencement of the first year of the reign of Zedekiah, king of Judah*" (1 Nephi 1:3 [1:4]), that the story of Lehi and his family begins.

LEHI'S LIFE THREATENED

The fact that Lehi and his family could read and write in the Egyptian language suggests that Lehi was probably a traveling merchant. Although he was Hebrew, he apparently bought, sold and traded goods in or near Jerusalem and Egypt. Lehi may have lived near the King's Highway which led south toward the Gulf of Aqaba and then west toward Egypt.

During "*the first year of the reign of Zedekiah*" (1 Nephi 1:3 [1:4]), Lehi had a very powerful and significant spiritual vision. Lehi's son, Nephi, wrote:

...after the Lord had shewn marvellous things unto my father Lehi, yea, concerning the destruction of Jerusalem, behold he went forth among the people and began to prophesy and to declare unto them concerning the things which he had both seen and heard. And it came to pass that the Jews did mock him because of the things which he testified of them; for he truly testified of their wickedness and their abominations...And when the Jews heard these things, they were angry with him...and they also sought his life, that they might take it away.

—1 Nephi 1:18–22 (1:18–20)

DEPARTURE INTO THE WILDERNESS

Warned by God that his life was being threatened, Lehi was directed to take his family and depart Jerusalem. Because of the quick departure, he left behind his worldly possessions and riches. He took his family, provisions, and tents into the wilderness (1 Nephi 1:29 [2:4]). His ability to quickly depart with all the necessary supplies provides further evidence that he was a traveling merchant who owned a camel caravan.[43, 44]

...and he came down by the borders near the shore of the Red Sea; and he did travel in the wilderness with his family, which consisted of my mother, Sariah, and my elder brothers, which were Laman, Lemuel and Sam. And it came to pass that when he had travelled three days in the

43 Verneil W. Simmons. *Peoples, Places and Prophecies.* Independence, MO: Zarahemla Research Foundation, 1986. p. 61

44 Glenn A. Scott. *Voices from the Dust: New Light on an Ancient American Record.* Marceline, MO, Walsworth Publishing Co., 2002. p. 67

wilderness, he pitched his tent in a valley beside a river of water.

—1 Nephi 1:30–33 (2:5–6)

It takes longer than three days to travel from Jerusalem to the Red Sea. Most likely, they were following the King's Highway which was in use even before the time of Moses (Num 20:17). As a traveling merchant, he would have been very familiar with this route. Consequently, they would not have considered themselves in the wilderness while on the King's Highway.

Where the King's Highway turns westward, Lehi's family entered the wilderness by heading south along the east side of the Gulf of Aqaba. They must have traveled along the East Coast of the Gulf of Aqaba or in the shade of nearby mountain valleys. "[A camel] *can carry large loads for up to 25 miles a day.*"[45] After three days and a distance of about seventy miles, they found a steadily flowing stream. One possibility is the valley known as *Wadi Tayyib Al-Ism* (The Valley of the Good Name). This valley:

---

45   "Arabian Camel" *NationalGeographic.com.* <https://www.nationalgeographic.com/animals/mammals/a/arabian-camel/> 23 Nov 2019.

winds its way for 2 km down to the sea. This part of the wadi [valley] *is quite spectacular. Its walls are 10 to 20 meters* [33-66 feet] *apart and rise about 100 meters* [330 feet] *above the wadi floor.*[46]

Thanks to the shade and the fresh water the temperature inside the canyon is always more pleasant than [a] *few meters away*[47]

Along with the shade and supply of freshwater, the associated narrow steep valley walls would also provide a good place to hide from wandering thieves.

Some believe that this may be where Lehi's family lived for a brief period. This is based on both the location and the description given in the Book of Mormon.[48]

> *And when my father* [Lehi] *saw that the waters of the river emptied into the fountain of the Red Sea* [Gulf of Aqaba], *he spake unto Laman, saying: O that thou mightest be like unto this river, continually running into the fountain of all righteousness. And he also spake unto Lemuel: O that thou mightest be like unto this valley, firm, and steadfast, and immovable in keeping the commandments of the Lord.*
>
> —1 Nephi 1:36–37 (2:8–9)

46   Virgil A. Treat and Robert F. Johnon. "Saudi Arabia Investigation Report (IR) SA-59." *United State Department of the Interior Geological Survey.* 1968. p. 2. <https://pubs.usgs.gov/of/1968/0277/report.pdf> 24 Jan 2020.

47   Florent Egal. "The Valley of Moses" *The Saudi Arabia Tourism Guide.* 5 Mar 2018. <http://www.saudiarabiatourismguide.com/tayeb-ism/ 23 Jan 2020.

48   George D. Potter. "A Candidate in Arabia for the 'Valley of Lemuel.'" *Book of Mormon Central.* 1999. <https://archive.bookofmormoncentral.org/content/new-candidate-ara-bia-"valley-lemuel"> 18 Sep 2019.

BACK TO JERUSALEM

The Plates of Brass

Once they were settled, the Lord spoke to Lehi in a dream.

...the Lord hath commanded me [Lehi] that thou [my son, Nephi,] and thy brethren shall return to Jerusalem. For behold, Laban hath the record of the Jews, and also a genealogy of my forefathers, and they are engraven upon the plates of brass. Wherefore the Lord hath commanded me that thou [Nephi] and thy brothers should go unto the house of Laban, and seek the records, and bring them down hither into the wilderness.

—1 Nephi 1:60–62 (3:32–34)

Such a record on metal plates must have been very sacred to the Jews. After arriving in Jerusalem, it was quickly understood that Laban would not easily hand them over. Laman had been the first one to approach Laban to request the brass plates. Laban cast him out and threatened to kill him. All of the brothers went to Laban on the next occasion. They offered to buy the plates with the riches their father had left behind. Laban responded by having them thrown out and kept their gold and silver. Laban then sent his servants to kill them. They quickly found a place to hide. Laman and Lemuel then took out their anger on their younger brothers. An angel appeared to them. After reprimanding Laman and Lemuel for the weakness of their faith, they were told that Laban would be delivered into their hands. Nephi then went alone into the city to speak with Laban. On the way, Nephi found him drunken and unconscious. The Lord directed Nephi to kill Laban. Nephi hesitated. The command was repeated two more times. Nephi was reminded of the threats to kill them, the fact that he had stolen their property, and was not obedient to the Lord's commandments. Nephi then received this insight:

> *Behold the Lord slayeth the wicked to bring forth his righteous purposes: it is better that one man should perish, than that a nation should dwindle and perish in unbelief. And now, when I, Nephi, had heard these words, I remembered the words of the Lord which he spake unto me in the wilderness, saying, that inasmuch as thy seed shall keep my commandments, they shall prosper in the land of promise.—Yea, and I also thought that they could not keep the commandments of the Lord according to the law of Moses, save they should have the law. And I also knew that the law was engraven upon the plates of brass.*
>
> —1 Nephi 1:114–118 (4:13–16)

At the Lord's command, he beheaded Laban with Laban's own sword. Then, with a bit of deception, Nephi was able to gain custody of those precious plates. They all returned to Lehi's campsite unharmed and bringing with them those sacred brass plates. Zoram, a servant of Laban, also came with them (1 Nephi 1:119–146 [4:17–5:1]).

The brass plates became their record of the teachings of the Jews. For centuries to come, those brass plates would be passed from generation to generation.

Wives for Lehi's Sons

Lehi was fully aware that his family would not be returning to Jerusalem and was concerned that his sons did not have wives. Lehi sent them to Ishmael, to ask him to bring his family so that they might accompany them on their journey.

> ...the Lord did soften the heart of Ishmael, and also his household, insomuch that they took their journey with us down into the wilderness to the tent of our father....I, Nephi, took one of the daughters of Ishmael to wife; and also my brethren took of the daughters of Ishmael to wife; and also, Zoram took the eldest daughter of Ishmael to wife.
>
> —1 Nephi 2:11; 5:7 (7:5; 16:7)

TRAVELING THE RED SEA COAST

The Round Ball

> ...the voice of the Lord spake unto my father...and commanded him, that on the morrow, he should take his journey into the wilderness....as my father arose in the morning...he beheld upon the ground a round ball, of curious workmanship; and it was of fine brass. And within the ball were two spindles; and the one pointed the way whither we should go into the wilderness.
>
> —1 Nephi 5:10–11 (16:9–10)

Many years later, Alma would describe this *round ball* to his son, Helaman:

> *...our fathers called it liahona, which is interpreted, a compass; and the Lord prepared it...to shew unto our fathers the course which they should travel in the wilderness; and it did work for them according to their faith in God.*
>
> —Alma 17:71–73 (37:38–40)

The liahona directed them southward, keeping to the more fertile areas where they could find food.

Shazer

Progress must have been slower for this larger group. Their numbers had more than doubled and they were traveling, in part, over some mountainous terrain. They covered a much shorter distance as they:

> *...travelled for the space of four days, nearly a south, southeast direction, and we did pitch our tents again; and we did call the name of the place Shazer.*
>
> —1 Nephi 5:15 (16:13).

Shazer is the name that they gave to this place. It would not have been known by that name to other travelers. Hugh Nibley states:

> The name is intriguing. The combination shajer is quite common in Palestinian place names; it is a collective meaning "trees," and many Arabs (especially in Egypt) pronounce it shazher....Lehi's people could hardly have picked a better name for their first suitable stopping place than Shazer.[49]

There is an oasis, *Wadi Agharr* (Beautiful Valley), which is several miles long and has many trees. It would have been a good place to rest and resupply the group with necessities.

Nephi Makes a Bow

After resting for a while, they continued their journey southward along the coast of the Red Sea.

> And it came to pass that we did travel for the space of many days, slaying food by the way, with our bows and arrows, and our stones, and our slings; and we did follow the directions of the ball, which led us in more fertile parts of the wilderness....after...we had travelled for the space of many days, we did pitch our tents...that we might again rest ourselves and obtain food for our families.
>
> —1 Nephi 5:19–21 (16:15–17)

However, misfortune and another test of their faith caught up with them. Nephi's bow broke. The bows of his brothers "*lost their*

---

49   Hugh Nibley. *Lehi in the Desert and the World of the Jaredites.* Salt Lake City, UT: Bookcraft, 1952. p. 90.

springs" (1 Nephi 5:26 [16:21]). As a result, they were hungry due to a lack of food. That is when Nephi:

> *...did make out of wood a bow, and out of a straight stick, an arrow; wherefore, I did arm myself with a bow and arrow, with a sling, and with stone*
>
> —1 Nephi 5:28 (16:23).

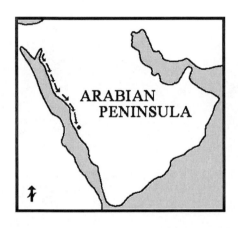

One ancient Arab tradition suggests that wood suitable for making a bow is nab wood. These trees can be found on Mt. Jasum and Mount Azd near the West Coast of the Arabian Peninsula.[50] Another possibility is Atim wood (olive tree) which grows at an elevation of about 6,000 feet, also in the mountains of the Arabian Peninsula.[51]

The question then became, where should Nephi go with his new bow to find food in this new and strange land? Lehi was told to look at the liahona. New writing on it gave directions to a nearby mountain (1 Nephi 5:30–41 [16:24–32]). After going to the top of that mountain, Nephi:

> *...did slay beasts, insomuch, that I did obtain food for our families.—And it came to pass that I did return to our tents, bearing the beasts which I had slain; and now,*

---

50   Ibid. pp. 66-68

51   George Potter and Richard Wellington. *Discovering the Lehi-Nephi Trail.* Unpublished manuscript. 2000. p. 141; *Step by Step Through the Book of Mormon, First Nephi 16:23* <https://stepbystep.alancminer.com/node/2229 > 7 Jun 2018.

when they beheld that I had obtained food, how great was
their joy.

—1 Nephi 5:37–40 (16:30–32)

Once they were rested and had plenty of food, they continued on their journey, according to the directions given on the liahona.

Nahom

And it came to pass that we did again take our journey, travelling nearly the same course as in the beginning; and after that we had travelled for the space of many days, we did pitch our tents again, that we might tarry for the space of a time. And it came to pass that Ishmael died and was buried in the place which was called Nahom.

—1 Nephi 5:42–44 (16:33–34)

Stopping here for a time suggests the availability of resources to again resupply their needs. It was also a place where they felt safe.

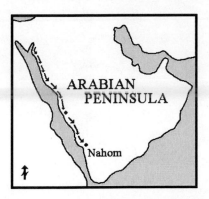

Notice that Nephi did not say they called the place Nahom. It was already known by that name. In 1999, a stone altar was found in an area of Yemen that had been a religious and cultural center from

2,000 B.C. to 500 B.C. Various altars were found that appear to have been symbolic gifts to celebrate distinct events. One particular altar refers to the tribal name of Nihm. Since early Hebrew writing used consonants and no vowels, Nihm and Nahom would be equivalent words—NHM. It has been estimated that the altar was constructed within a few decades of when Lehi and his family passed through this area.[52]

The "*Hebrew root NHM is found repeatedly in the Bible and relates to sorrow, hunger, consoling, and mourning.*"[53] Nihm (or Nahom) would have been a burial place.

TURNING EASTWARD

Eastward From Nahom

> *...we did again take our journey in the wilderness; and we did travel nearly eastward, from that time forth. And we did travel and wade through much affliction in the wilderness; and our women did bear children in the wilderness. And so great were the blessings of the Lord upon us, that while we did live upon the raw meat in the wilderness, our women did give plenty of suck for their children, and were strong, yea, even like unto the men; and they began to bear the journeyings without murmurings... And if it so be that the children of men keep the commandments of God, he doth nourish them, and strengthen*

---

52   S. Kent Brown. "New Light—'The Place That Was Called Nahom': New Light from Ancient Yemen." *Journal of Book of Mormon Studies*, Vol. 8, no. 1, 1999. p. 68.

53   David Damrosch. *The Narrative Covenant: Transformations of Genre in the Growth of Biblical Literature.* San Francisco, CA: Harper and Row, 1987. pp. 128-129.

them, and provide means whereby they can accomplish the
thing which he hath commanded them....

—1 Nephi 5:55–59 (17:1–3)

The Lord may have directed them to eat raw meat so that the smoke from cooking fires would not attract thieves.

Sojourn For Eight Years

...he [the Lord] *did provide means for us while we did sojourn in the wilderness. And we did sojourn for the space of many years, yea, even eight years in the wilderness.*

—1 Nephi 5:61 (17:4)

Sojourn means to temporarily stop traveling and to live in one area for a time. They felt safe. By settling down for a while, the anxieties and frustrations of their journey could be put aside and the death of Ishmael could be accepted. Much like the early Hebrews who are believed to have wandered this same peninsula for forty years, Lehi's family was able to find food and water. For this, like the Hebrews of old, they gave credit to the Lord.

It was during these eight years that Lehi had two more sons, Jacob and Joseph.

Land Bountiful

And we did come to the land which we called Bountiful, because of its much fruit, and also, wild honey; and all these things were prepared of the Lord, that we might not perish.—And we beheld the Sea, which we called Irreantum, which being interpreted, is, many waters. And

it came to pass that we did pitch our tents by the seashore;
and notwithstanding we had suffered many afflictions and
much difficulty, yea, even so much that we cannot write
them all, we were exceedingly rejoiced when we came to
the seashore; and we called the place Bountiful, because of
its much fruit.

—1 Nephi 5:62–67 (17:5–6)

One may ask why Nephi uses the word "Irreantum" and then provides a translation. If this was written for fellow Hebrews, it would not be necessary. One source suggests:

…if Irreantum is a South Semitic name, it could be com-
posed of irr-an plus –tum. These words would form a two-
noun construct chain that would mean something like
"watering of completeness" or "watering of (super) abun-
dance," a meaning that is compatible with the translation
"many waters."[54]

"*Many waters*" and "*seashore*" are apparent references to the Indian Ocean.

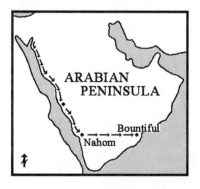

54   Paul Y. Hoskisson, Brian M. Hauglid, and John Gee. "What's in a Name? Irreantum."
      Journal of Book of Mormon Studies, Vol. 11, No. 1, 2002. pp. 92-93

There is a small oasis along the southern coast of the Arabian Peninsula that was unknown to the Western world when the Book of Mormon was published. Today, this oasis is called Salalah. The area is an Arabian resort providing relief from the hot desert. During the monsoon season, July to September, rain is plentiful.

Some peculiarity in the shape of these mountains draws the monsoon clouds…which are in consequence covered with mist and rain throughout the summer… All the way along the south Arabian coast for 1400 miles…only these twenty miles get a regular rainfall… Massive tamarinds [hardwood trees that produce a tropical fruit] *grow in the valleys and on the downs, great fig trees rise above the wind-rippled grass… To the south were green meadows… thickets and spreading trees, whereas a stone's throw to the north was empty desert—sand, rocks and a few wisps of withered grass… To the south grassy downs, green jungles, and shadowy gorges fell away to the plain of Jarbib and to the Indian Ocean.*[55]

The Construction of a Ship

And it came to pass that the Lord spake unto me [Nephi], saying: Thou shalt construct a ship, after the manner which I shall shew thee, that I may carry thy people across these waters.

—1 Nephi 5:70 (17:8)

---

55   William Thesiger. *Arabian Sands.* London: Penguin Classics. 1959. pp. 47–48, 83. <https://books.google.com/books?id=SH6crRdP9sUC&pg> 28 Jul 2018.

The construction of a ship entailed finding the materials, including ore to make tools. Nephi's brothers, Laman and Lemuel, began to ridicule him for believing that he could build a ship. In response, he reprimanded them by reciting to them the many ways in which the Lord had blessed their people—beginning with the time of Moses. He reminded them that they had seen an angel. The brothers reacted with anger. Nephi warned them that he was doing what the Lord had commanded.

> ...the Lord said unto me [Nephi], *Stretch forth thine hand...unto thy brethren, and...I will shock them, saith the Lord; and this will I do, that they may know that I am the Lord their God. ...I stretched forth my hand unto my brethren, and...the Lord did shake them, even according to the word which he had spoken.*
>
> —1 Nephi 5:163–164 (17:53–54)

Laman and Lemuel were quick to repent. They then worked together, carefully following the directions of the Lord, and the ship was completed.

CROSSING THE PACIFIC OCEAN

Departure by Ship

> ...the voice of the Lord came unto my father [Lehi], *that we should arise and go down into the ship. ...after that we had prepared all things, much fruits and meat from the wilderness, and honey in abundance, and provisions, according to that which the Lord had commanded us, we did go down into the ship with all our loading and our*

seeds, and whatsoever thing we had brought with us. ...
we did put forth into the sea, and were driven forth before
the wind, towards the promised land...

—1 Nephi 5:175–181 (18:5–8)

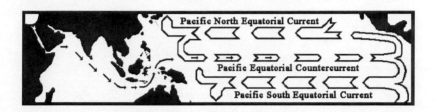

At certain times of the year, monsoon winds blow south from Arabia and the Persian Gulf directly toward India and the islands beyond. These winds reverse themselves several months later. As Lehi's family were probably not very knowledgeable in sailing or navigation, they had to rely on the directions of the Lord. They most likely departed in the early summer when the winds would have carried them eastward.

Driven Back Four Days

After many days, Laman, Lemuel and the sons of Ishmael and their wives began to treat the voyage like a party, dancing and singing while being very rude to the others. Nephi began to worry that the Lord would become angry with them. In the middle of the ocean, he knew they were very vulnerable. When Nephi tried to warn his brothers, they tied him with cords.

...after they had bound me, insomuch that I could not
move, the compass, which had been prepared of the Lord,
did cease to work...they knew not whither they should

steer the ship, insomuch, that there arose a great storm, yea, a great and terrible tempest; and we were driven back upon the waters for the space of three days.

—1 Nephi 5:190–192 (18:12–13)

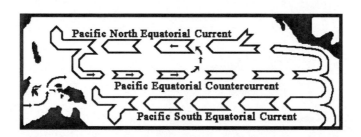

Between the two westward-flowing equatorial currents is a very narrow eastward-flowing countercurrent. The narrowness of that current makes it difficult to sail, especially without good navigation equipment. Besides, the winds are more gentle. Going off course, north or south, would increase the chances of encountering stormy turbulent weather that would easily carry a ship back toward the west. During the summer months, the westward North Equatorial Current is often the location of tropical depressions and typhoons or hurricanes.

After…we had been driven back upon the waters for the space of four days, my brethren began to see that the judgment of God was upon them and that they must perish, save that they should repent of their iniquities…wherefore, they came unto me and loosed the bands which was upon my wrists, and behold, they had much swollen, exceedingly; and also, mine ancles were much swollen… after they had loosed me…I took the compass, and it did work whither I desired it…I prayed unto the Lord; and after…I had prayed, the winds did cease, and the storm

did cease, and there was a great calm...I, Nephi, did guide
the ship, that we sailed again toward the promised land.

—1 Nephi 5:197–198, 209–211 (18:15, 21–22)

Arrival in the Promised Land

...after we had sailed for the space of many days, we did
arrive to the promised land...

—1 Nephi 5:212 (18:23)

The Pacific equatorial countercurrent could have easily brought
them ashore on the tropical west coast of Central America—probably
along the Pacific coast of Guatemala. It is believed that they initially
settled in the highlands of Guatemala and Southern Mexico.

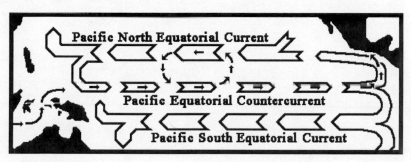

CONCLUSION

Events described in the Bible and Book of Mormon combined with archaeology, geography, and oceanography provide one compatible account. Taken together, all of this complements and supports the description of Lehi's journey provided in the Book of Mormon. I believe that these were...

REAL PEOPLE IN REAL PLACES!

CHAPTER 4:

THE MULEKITE CONNECTIONS

Introduction

After Lehi and his family arrived in this promised land, the animosity between Nephi and his older brothers continued. Eventually, they separated into two groups. The more righteous group was called Nephites, and the rebellious group was called Lamanites. Four hundred years later, their descendants were still dealing with this animosity. The Nephite King Mosiah, the elder:

> *...being warned of the Lord that he should flee... and as many as would hearken unto the voice of the Lord, should also depart out of the land with him, into the wilderness...And they departed out of the land into the wilderness...And they were admonished continually by the word of God; and they were led by the power of his arm, through the wilderness, until they came down into the land which is called the land of Zarahemla.*

—Mosiah 1:20–23 (1:12–13)

When the Nephites arrived in the lowlands, they discovered a group of people more familiarly known to us as the Mulekites. The term, "Mulekites," is not used anywhere in the Book of Mormon. The term has been used when referring to those associated with the descendants of Mulek. Within the Book of Mormon, these people were referred to as the people of Zarahemla.

The Mulekites, according to their traditions, had departed Jerusalem at the end of the reign of King Zedekiah and knew that Jerusalem had been destroyed. For the Nephites, this was confirmation of Lehi's prophecies regarding Jerusalem.

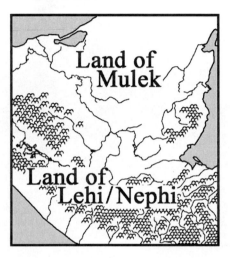

Now the land south was called Lehi, and the land north was called Mulek, which was after the son of Zedekiah; for the Lord did bring Mulek into the land north, and Lehi into the land south.

—Helaman 2:129 (6:10)[56]

---

56   The 1830 edition reads: "after the sons of Zedekiah." That would suggest that more than one son survived the downfall of Jerusalem and was brought to the Americas. It was a typesetting error in the 1830 edition. It was discovered after the RLDS Church obtained a copy of the printer's manuscript and was corrected in their 1908 edition. Many subsequent editions of the Book of Mormon have also made this same correction.

This history of the Mulekites raises an interesting question. If, according to the Bible the sons of Zedekiah were slain (Jer. 39:5–7), how did a son of Zedekiah end up in America? The solution to this puzzle becomes a three-part endeavor to connect a seafaring people with the Mulekites:

1) Bible/Phoenician Connection,

2) Phoenician/Mayan Connection, and

3) Book of Mormon/Phoenician/Mayan Connection.

BIBLE/PHOENICIAN CONNECTION

Ebed-Melech

In 597 B.C., Zedekiah was placed on the throne as a puppet king under the Babylonian King, Nebuchadnezzar. Zedekiah was required to take an oath of allegiance to this king. However, Zedekiah favored a continuing close relationship with Egypt rather than submitting to the demands of King Nebuchadnezzar. His rebellious attitude toward Nebuchadnezzar was encouraged by his princes and the Phoenician King of Tyre, a very close ally.

Jeremiah had been prophesying to King Zedekiah that he should submit to the demands of King Nebuchadnezzar of Babylon. However, Jeremiah's enemies convinced Zedekiah to throw Jeremiah into a dungeon. "*They lowered Jeremiah by ropes into the cistern; it had no water in it, only mud, and Jeremiah sank down into the mud*" *(Jer. 38:6, NRSV).* In that pit, Jeremiah was doomed to die.

After hearing of Jeremiah's potential fate, Ebed-Melech told King Zedekiah that the men who had put Jeremiah into the dungeon had acted wickedly (Jer. 38:7–9).

*Then the king commanded Ebed-Melech the Ethiopian,
"Take three men with you from here, and pull the prophet
Jeremiah up from the cistern before he dies."*

—Jer. 38:10, NRSV

Notice that the king did not send any men, but simply told
Ebed-Melech to take the men that he would need. Ebed-Melech had
sufficient authority to personally oversee this effort.

*So Ebed-Melech took the men with him and went to the
house of the king, to a wardrobe of the storehouse, and
took from there old rags and worn-out clothes, which he
let down to Jeremiah in the cistern by ropes. Then Ebed-
Melech the Ethiopian said to Jeremiah, "Just put the rags
and clothes between your armpits and the ropes." Jeremiah
did so. Then they drew Jeremiah up by the ropes and
pulled him out of the cistern. And Jeremiah remained in
the court of the guard.*

—Jer. 38:11–13, NRSV

In Hebrew, Melech means king. Ebed-Melech means servant of
the king. It was his title. He was described as a court official assigned to
the royal palace. Ebed-Melech is also referred to as a saris, a term that
has been translated as eunuch, official or military officer (Jer. 38:7).
Only the context determines the intended meaning.

*Ebed-Melech's bold public confrontation of Zedekiah,
followed by Zedekiah's compliance, indicates that Ebed-
Melech had considerable clout. The most plausible*

explanation is that Ebed-Melech was a high-ranking military officer."[57]

After Jeremiah's rescue, he was confined to the court of the guard, as though imprisoned for his protection. Jeremiah remained there until after Jerusalem was conquered. It is likely that Ebed-Melech, as a court official and military officer, was in charge of that court of the guard.

The word of the Lord came to Jeremiah while he was confined in the court of the guard: Go and say to Ebed-Melech the Ethiopian: Thus says the Lord of hosts, the God of Israel: I am going to fulfill my words against this city for evil and not for good, and they shall be accomplished in your presence on that day. But I will save you on that day, says the Lord, and you shall not be handed over to those whom you dread. For I will surely save you, and you shall not fall by the sword; but you shall have your life as a prize of war, because you have trusted in me, says the Lord.

—Jer. 39:15–18, NRSV

Zedekiah eventually began to openly rebel against King Nebuchadnezzar. As a result, Nebuchadnezzar laid siege to Jerusalem. When supplies and food began to dwindle, King Zedekiah and some of his men tried to flee. However, they were captured and brought before Nebuchadnezzar. Zedekiah's reign ended with his capture around 587–586 B.C.

---

57   J. Daniel Hays. "Black Soldiers." *Bible Review,* Vol. 14, no. 4 Aug 1998. p. 50.

> [King Nebuchadnezzar] *of Babylon slaughtered the sons of Zedekiah…before his eyes; also the king of Babylon slaughtered all the nobles of Judah. He put out the eyes of Zedekiah and bound him in fetters to take him to Babylon.*
>
> —Jer. 39:6–7, NRSV

King Nebuchadnezzar recognized the fact that Jeremiah tried to support his efforts to rule over Jerusalem. As such, he allowed Jeremiah to go free. He also told his captain to grant any request of Jeremiah (Jer. 39:11–13). Ebed-Melech may have been granted safe passage at Jeremiah's request.

The Surviving Son of Zedekiah

It is apparent in the Book of Mormon that the Mulekite traditions included an awareness of Nebuchadnezzar's cruel murder of Zedekiah's sons.

> *And now will ye dispute that Jerusalem was destroyed? Will ye say that the sons of Zedekiah were not slain, all except it were Mulek? Yea, and do ye not behold that the seed of Zedekiah are with us, and that they were driven out of the land of Jerusalem?*
>
> —Helaman 3:56–57 (8:21)

The *"seed of Zedekiah"* is among the Mulekites? How could he have survived and how did he come to the Americas?

In the Biblical descriptions of the final confrontation between Zedekiah and Nebuchadnezzar, the frequent use of the word "all" is interesting. According to the Bible, 2 Kings 25 (NRSV) and Jeremiah 39 (NRSV), Nebuchadnezzar and "***all** his army*" laid a siege around

Jerusalem. Zedekiah and "*__all__ his army*" tried to escape. "*__All__ the houses of Jerusalem*" were burned down. "*__All__ the army of the Chaldeans*" helped to break down the walls around Jerusalem. Nebuchadnezzar "*slaughtered __all__ the nobles of Judah.*" However, in both Old Testament books, the statement is made that the "sons of Zedekiah" were slaughtered. The word "all" is noticeably absent. This leaves open the possibility of a surviving male heir.

> On biblical precedent, a male infant…would be excluded as a "son" of Zedekiah. [The Bible]…could have been technically correct in reporting that the "sons" of Zedekiah were beheaded even though a male heir might have been left alive.[58]

Infant mortality was higher in those days. Newborn infants were placed in a nursery. A baby that survived early childhood would later be moved to the palace. That is when a young boy would become recognized as a son of the king. A small child would have been easy to hide from Nebuchadnezzar's wrath.

If a young child was to find his way to the Americas, a guardian or escort would be needed. The promise given to Ebed-Melech by Jeremiah that he would be saved, coupled with his being a servant of the king, means that he would have been aware of the inner workings of Zedekiah's family. He may have taken charge of Zedekiah's nursery to protect the young children. Perhaps he had affectionate feelings for them and knew their lives were in danger. Ebed-Melech may have then chosen to escape northward with his charges toward Hazor. It

---

58   Verneil W. Simmons. *Peoples, Places and Prophecies.* Independence, MO: Zarahemla Research Foundation, 1986. p. 95.

is about ninety miles north of Jerusalem—about four to five days by camel caravan.

Word may have then reached Ebed-Melech that Jeremiah also prophesied of the destruction of Hazor.

> *Flee, wander far away, hide in deep places, O inhabitants of Hazor! says the Lord. For King Nebuchadnezzar of Babylon has made a plan against you and formed a purpose against you"*

—Jer. 49:30 NRSV

The threat against Hazor may have been the approaching army of Nebuchadnezzar. They would have been headed toward Tyre. The king of Tyre was facing retaliation for encouraging Zedekiah to rebel

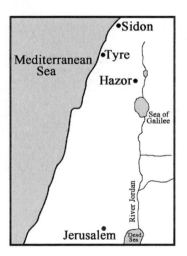

against Nebuchadnezzar. In the same year that Jerusalem was defeated, Nebuchadnezzar started his siege of Tyre. By the time that Ebed-Melech would have arrived in Phoenicia, the siege of Tyre was being planned or already in effect. Ebed-Melech may have then led those who were with him further north to Sidon. From Hazor, that would have been an additional two days by camel caravan.

The Phoenicians

The Phoenicians and the Israelites had been very close allies for many years. At that time, the Phoenicians and the Israelites:

...spoke the same language and wrote in the same script. Even their religion was similar... The Phoenicians and the Israelites built Jerusalem together...they went on joint trading expeditions... They never went to war against each other.[59]

Sidon was the site of a major Phoenician port from which goods were transported throughout the Mediterranean. With seafaring Phoenicians and the availability of the sea, seeking safety could have meant simply launching a ship toward a distant land. They knew that King Nebuchadnezzar could not follow. The best security would be to flee to a land unknown to the rest of the civilized world but very well known to the Phoenicians.

Since the Phoenicians and Jews were close allies, any child of King Zedekiah would be given a priority. As an official in Zedekiah's court, Ebed-Melech may have personally known some of the leaders in Phoenicia. Either case would allow Ebed-Melech and his companions safe passage to a destination far from Nebuchadnezzar. With their precious cargo, they probably headed for a familiar but secret destination. Isaiah referred to Phoenicians as a people "*whose feet* [ships] *carried her to settle far away*" (Isa. 23:7 NRSV).

There was no fear of the Phoenicians losing the secrecy of their route. If or when they did return, any non-Phoenician passengers would have been left behind. Any Phoenician sailor who chose to disclose their route would be put to death. The extreme secrecy coupled with the eventual downfall of the Phoenician empire led to the temporary loss of any knowledge of the western hemisphere.

---

59   Ephraim Stern. "Phoenicia and Its Special Relationship with Israel." *Biblical Archaeology* Vol. 43, No. 6. Nov/Dec 2017. p. 40.

PHOENICIAN/MAYAN CONNECTION

A Land with Navigable Rivers

The Phoenicians had a history of establishing colonies at various distant locations. "*Sicilian historian, Diodorus, writing in the first century BC, '…in the deep off Africa is an island of considerable size… The Phoenicians had discovered it by accident after having planted many colonies throughout Africa.'*"[60]

The Phoenicians were aware of a land beyond the Pillars of Heracles (the Rock of Gibraltar), west of Africa, and with "*navigable rivers.*"[61] This could only be the Americas. Once discovered, the Phoenicians would have then exploited this secret location by establishing distant colonies. One of those early colonies may have been established along the coast of the Yucatan Peninsula, beginning perhaps a century or more before the time of Nebuchadnezzar.

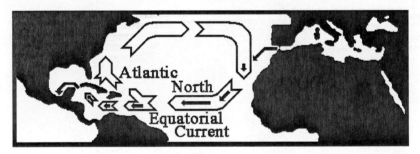

---

60   Nick Vulich. *History Bytes: 37 People, Places, and Events That Shaped American History.* Digital History Project. Lulu.com. 2015. p. 3. <https://books.google.com/books?id=iNgNCgAAQBAJ&pg=PA3&lpg=PA3&dq=%22in+the+deep+off+Africa+is+an+island+of+considerable+size> 10 Jul 2019.

61   *The Library of History of Diodorus Siculus, Vol. III.* Loeb Classical Library edition, 1939. p. 19–20 <http://penelope.uchicago.edu/Thayer/E/Roman/Texts/Diodorus_Siculus/5B*.html> 17 Aug 2019.

From Plato, 360 B.C.: *This power came forth out of the Atlantic Ocean, for in those days the Atlantic was navigable; and there was an island situated in front of the straits which are by you called the Pillars of Heracles* [Rock of Gibralter]*; the island was larger than Libya and Asia put together, and was the way to other islands, and from these you might pass to the whole of the opposite continent which surrounded the true ocean; for this sea which is within the Straits of Heracles is only a harbour, having a narrow entrance, but that other is a real sea, and the surrounding land may be most truly called a boundless continent.*[62]

...following the old track of Phoenician navigators in their exploration of the coast of Africa, and striking westward into the great equatorial drift current around the southern border of the Sargasso Sea, we land at the point of Yucatan, the pivotal point off which the current makes a turn to sweep into the Gulf of Mexico, we come upon colossal ruins of ancient date which, with the addition of the admixture of eastern Asiatic elements, could hardly be better described than in the words of M. Lenormant in regard to the monuments of the Phoenicians.[63]

---

62   "English Translations of Plato's Atlantis Dialogues, Benjamin Jowett 1871." *Atlanta-Scout.* <https://www.atlantis-scout.de/atlantis_timaeus_critias.htm#jowett> 10 Jul 2019.

63   Alexander MacWhorter. "Tammuz and the Mound Builders" *The Galaxy*, Vol. 14. Jul to Dec 1872. p. 93. <https://books.google.com/books?id=cTGgAAAAMAAJ&pg=PA93&lpg=PA93&dq> 22 Sep 2018.

Mythical Twins

In my research regarding the Maya, I repeatedly encountered stories of legendary twins associated with the underworld. These myths were associated with numerous caves of Mexico and particularly the deeper parts of those caves. The source of that legend concerned me until I stumbled upon a similar legend common in the Middle East.

Throughout the Mediterranean, there are varying stories of legendary hero twins. They were often referred to as Castor and Pollux. They allegedly had the same mother but different fathers. Castor's father was the king of Sparta and, therefore, mortal. Pollux, as the son of Zeus, was immortal.

> *They were great warriors and were noted for their devotion to each other. In one version of the legend, after Castor was killed...Pollux...begged Zeus to allow his brother to share his immortality with him. Zeus arranged for the twins to divide their time evenly between Hades and Heaven, and in their honor, he created the constellation Gemini.*[64]

These twins were both considered guardians of mankind. This was especially true of sailors, such as the Phoenicians. These mythical twins would appear to them as St. Elmo's Fire, an electrical phenomenon seen at the top of a mast during a thunderstorm. It was considered a sign of good luck and protection for the sailors.

In the New World, the mythical hero twins, Xbalanque and Hunahpu, are said to have been worshiped by the early Mayans. Detailed

---

[64] "Castor and Pollux." *The Columbia Encyclopedia*, 6th ed. *Encyclopedia.com.* <https://www.encyclopedia.com/literature-and-arts/classical-literature-mythology-and-folklore/folklore-and-mythology/castor-and-pollux> 23 Sep 2019.

knowledge of them comes primarily from the Popol Vuh. When comparing these two legends, one can find some striking similarities.

Both Mayan and Old World twin legends involved twin boys...

- who had supernatural powers.

- who were associated with stories of the underworld.

- who, in different ways, suffered death and were restored to life.

- who, as Mayan twins, became the sun and moon; and as Old World twins became the two brightest stars in the constellation Gemini, and yet symbolized night and day.

- who modeled good behavior defending mankind.

- who were associated with sports. This is especially true of the Mayan twins.

Stories of mythical twins found in a land with navigable rivers beyond the Straits of Gibraltar supports the suggestion that the Phoenicians, the ocean-going merchants of a bygone era, had connections to the Americas.

BOOK OF MORMON/PHOENICIAN/MAYAN CONNECTION

The Arrival of the Mulekites

Based on the above, it is estimated that the Mulekites may have arrived in the Americas as early as 586–585 B.C. It is stated that the area, later known as the land of Desolation, *"was discovered by the people of Zarahemla* [the Mulekites]*; it being the place of their first landing"* (Alma 13:74 [22:30]). Upon their arrival, the Mulekites may have briefly come ashore in the vicinity of the Grijalva River near La Venta (Land of Moron). The Phoenicians may have had previous encounters with the Olmec/Jaredites and recognized that this was not their destination. They must have then sailed their ships eastward along the coast toward the mouth of the Usumacinta River. Their guests were then given their freedom in this new world.

Such a journey across the Atlantic Ocean in a sailing vessel would have taken about two months.

> *Behold, it came to pass that Mosiah discovered that the people of Zarahemla, came out from Jerusalem, at the time that Zedekiah, king of Judah, was carried away captive into Babylon. And they journied in the wilderness, and was brought by the hand of the Lord, across the great waters, into the land where Mosiah discovered them; and they had dwelt there from that time forth.*
>
> —Omni 1:26–27 (1:15–16)

River Sidon

Sidon was a major port city in Phoenicia. Regardless of their origin, "*Phoenicians referred to themselves as Sidonians.*"[65]

In the Book of Alma, the waters of Sidon or river Sidon is frequently mentioned. The name Sidon is probably not a coincidence but a name given to the river by Phoenician settlers. This river Sidon is used to refer to boundaries between different portions of the land (Alma 1:70 [2:15]), location of a battle (Alma 1:84, 92 [2:27, 35]), or a place of baptism (Alma 2:4 [4:4]).

---

65   Barry Amundsen. *Phoenix, Phoenicians, Tyre and Sidon today and destiny, (remembering David Flynn).* 11 Apr 2012. <http://www.fivedoves.com/letters/apr2012/barrya411-2.htm> 22 Feb 2020.

...Alma departed from [the land of Zarahemla], *and took his journey over into the land of Melek, on the west of the river Sidon, on the west, by the borders of the wilderness; And he began to teach the people in the land of Melek...the people came to him throughout all the borders of the land which was by the wilderness side.*

—Alma 6:4–6 (8:3–6)

The river Sidon was a dividing line between the land of Zarahemla and the land of Melek. The people of Zarahemla (Mulekites) may have named this river in memory of their origin.

Mulok, Melek or Mulek

- In the Book of Mosiah, there is a reference to a descendant of **Mulok** (11:78 [25:2])

- In the Book of Alma, there are several references to the land of **Melek** (6:4,5,7; 16:83, 254; 21:20 [8:3,4,5; 31:6; 32:28; 45:18])

- In the Book of Alma, there are multiple references to the city of **Mulek** (23:32; 24:2-59 [52:26; 52:2-34; 53:2, 6])

- In the Book of Helaman, there is a reference to the city of **Mulek** (2:77 [5:15]); the land of **Mulek** (2:129 [6:10]); and to **Mulek,** the son of Zedekiah (3:56 [8:21]).

Recall Ebed-Melech's name meant servant of the king. This was his title and not his name. Mulek (king) may have become the title of Zedekiah's surviving son and selected heirs.

If these names, Mulok/Melek/Mulek, are referring to the title of a Mulekite leader, why are there three different spellings? The early Hebrew language was written using only consonants. There were no vowels. Over time, people may have easily begun using different vowels while retaining the same consonant spelling. It is also possible that different regional dialects had developed. These slight differences in spelling may still be referring to the title of a Mulekite leader or the land or city in which he had once lived.

City of Mulek

Several cities, including "...*the city of Mulek...were on the east borders, by the seashore*" (Alma 23:32 [52:26]). Eastern borders suggest that the city may have been along the eastern side of the Yucatan Peninsula. Its title suggests that it may have been where this revered son of Zedekiah or his descendants settled for a time.

Land of Melek

> *The two primary Yaxchilan Emblem Glyphs usually occur together.... The Maya name for this main sign is Muluc. The translation of this main sign was given by the Maya to the Spanish at the time of the Conquest.*[66]

The glyph can now be read phonetically.

It may be no coincidence that the Mayan city of Yaxchilan is associated with a sign interpreted to mean Muluc. The second glyph may have been introduced at the time when the Nephites became the dominant part of the culture.

---

66   Neil Simmons and Ray Treat. "Maya Hieroglyphs Point to the Book of Mormon," *The Zarahemla Record*, 19–21. Winter, Spring & Summer, 1983. p. 3.

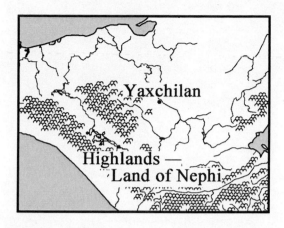

It is interesting to note the coincidence that this Mayan city, Yaxchilan, associated with this Muluc glyph, was on the western side of the Usumacinta River. The land of Melek was described as being on the western side of the river Sidon (Alma 6:4 [8:3]). This would suggest that the Usumacinta River is the Book of Mormon river Sidon. Yaxchilan is about 150 miles from the Gulf of Mexico. The "land of Melek" should not be confused with the "city of Mulek" which was closer to the seashore (Alma 24:27 [52:22]).

> There is a city of Mulek in the Book of Mormon but it does not meet the geographic requirements for Yaxchilan (Alma 24:27–29 [52:22–23]), Yaxchilan was a regional capital and was located on the west bank of a major river. The only city in the Book of Mormon that fits both of these requirements is the city of Zarahemla. Zarahemla was the capital of the Nephite lands (Helaman 1:29 [1:27]) and thus an important regional center...In summary, it appears that Yaxchilan is the Book of Mormon city of Zarahemla

which was the capital city of the land which was once known as the land of Mulek.[67]

The Nephites Discover the Mulekites

About four centuries after the arrival of the Mulekites in the lowlands, the Nephites were driven out of the highlands by the Lamanites. They were led by their religious leader, Mosiah.

> *And* [the Nephites] *were admonished continually by the word of God; and they were led by the power of His arm, through the wilderness, until they came down into the land which is called the land of Zarahemla.*
>
> —Omni 1:23 (1:13)

When mention is made of people traveling down into the land of Zarahemla, it is referring to a difference in elevation. They were traveling from the highlands to the lowlands of Southern Mexico. The forests between the highlands and the lowlands have been described as *"a swath of seemingly impenetrable terrain, crisscrossed by un-navigable rivers and barely accessible on foot."*[68] The simplest means of navigation in an impenetrable terrain is to follow a stream as it flows downward. Even though a stream is un-navigable by boat, it could still be followed by a group of people working together.

It is suggested here that the stream that they followed was part of the headwaters of the Usumacinta River or river Sidon.

---

67   Ibid. p. 4

68   Angela M. H. Schuster. "Traders of the Maya." *Archaeology*, Vol. 62, No. 4. Jul/Aug 2009. p. 14.

Now there were not so many of those descendants of Nephi, as they were of the people of Zarahemla, which was a descendant of Mulok, and those which came with him into the wilderness"

—Mosiah 11:78 (25:2).

And at the time that [the Nephite] *Mosiah* [I][69] *discovered…*[the Mulekites], *they had become exceeding numerous. Nevertheless…their language had become corrupted; and they had brought no records with them; and they denied the being of their Creator, and Mosiah, nor the people of Mosiah, could not understand them. But it came to pass that Mosiah caused that they should be taught in his language. And it came to pass that after they were taught in the language of Mosiah, Zarahemla gave a genealogy of his fathers, according to his memory…*

—Omni 1:28–33 (1:17–18)

For the language to have been "corrupted" means that it was not a different language. There were still some similarities, yet it had been somehow altered. It is assumed here that the Mulekites were brought here by the Phoenicians. In the beginning, the Phoenician language was identical to the Hebrew language. However, there is a tendency for any language to gradually change over time. The corruption probably refers to four centuries of ever-accumulating small changes in the language among both the Nephites and Mulekites. In addition, the Mulekite language may have been influenced by a trade relationship

---

69   For simplicity and clarity, in selected cases, Mosiah, the elder is referred to as Mosiah I and his grandson Mosiah, the younger, is referred to as Mosiah II.

with the Jaredites. Some Jaredite words and phrases probably became part of the Mulekite culture. Teaching the people of Zarahemla the language of Mosiah would not have taken a long time due to basic linguistic similarities.

It is interesting to note that the Mulekites "*had brought no records with them*" (Omni 1:30 [1:17]). This would explain why, after four centuries, their faith had dwindled to the point that "*...they denied the being of their Creator*" (Omni 1:31 [1:17]). In hindsight, this illustrates the wisdom of the Lord when He had Lehi send his sons back to Jerusalem to retrieve the brass plates. It was the scriptures in those brass plates that had helped the Nephites hold fast to their faith in God.

> *And it came to pass that the people of Zarahemla, and of Mosiah did unite together; and Mosiah was appointed to be their king.*

> —Omni 1:34 (1:19)

CONCLUSION

Events described in the Bible and Book of Mormon combined with the histories and legends of the Mayans and Phoenicians provide us with one compatible account. Taken together, all of this complements and supports the descriptions of the Mulekites as it is related to us in the Book of Mormon. I believe these were...

REAL PEOPLE IN REAL PLACES!

CCCCCCCCCCCCCCCCCCCCCCCCCC

CHAPTER 5:

ZENIFF'S COLONY

CCCCCCCCCCCCCCCCCCCCCCCCCC

Introduction

Four centuries after the arrival of Lehi and his family in the high-lands, persecution between the Nephite and Lamanites became intoler-able. Guided by the Lord, the Nephites fled from the land of Nephi. It is believed that they followed the headwaters of the Usumacinta River, the Book of Mormon's River Sidon, down to the lowlands where they discovered the people of Zarahemla, the Mulekites.

One group of Nephites was chosen to return to their homeland as spies, led by a man named Zeniff. They were sent by King Mosiah, the elder. The first attempt failed. Zeniff returned to Zarahemla and led a second group of people back to that same Lamanite territory. He was able to establish a peace treaty with the Lamanites. The Lamanites designated a specific part of their land where Zeniff and his people would be allowed to live peacefully.

After many years, the animosity between the Nephites and the Lamanites returned. One group of Nephites escaped back to Zarahemla. Another group searched unsuccessfully for an escape route. The discov-ery of their colony by another group of Nephites sent from the city of Zarahemla allowed them to finally escape from their persecution.

Understanding their struggles contributes greatly to the understanding of the geography where they lived.

ZENIFF RETURNS TO THE LAND OF NEPHI

Zeniff's First Attempt

Zeniff was the leader of a large group of Nephites chosen to go back to the land of Nephi to spy on the Lamanites. From Yaxchilan (city of Zarahemla) they probably followed the Usumacinta River (River Sidon) upstream.

Zeniff is described as a "*mighty man, and a stiffnecked man*" (Omni 1:50 [1:28]). After reaching their destination and observing the Lamanites, Zeniff wrote: "*I saw that which was good among them, I was desirous that they should not be destroyed*" (Mosiah 6:2–3 [9:1–2]). Some of those who had traveled with him strongly disagreed. An internal battle resulted in the deaths of many and only fifty survivors remained (Omni 1:50 [1:28]).

After a failed mission, the survivors, including Zeniff, returned to the city of Zarahemla (Yaxchilan).

Zeniff's Second Attempt

> *And yet, I* [Zeniff] *being over zealous to inherit the land of our fathers, collected as many as were desirous to go up to possess the land, and started again on our journey into the wilderness, to go up to the land; but we were smitten with famine and sore afflictions: for we were slow to remember the Lord our God.*
>
> —Mosiah 6:6 (9:3)

They believed that the weakness in their faith resulted in multiple difficulties and extra days wandering in the wilderness. However, eventually, they came to the same place where the previous group had fought.

Upon their arrival in the land of Nephi, Zeniff went to visit the Lamanite king. He successfully worked out an agreement so that his group would be allowed to live peacefully in "*the land of Lehi-Nephi, and the land of Shilom*" (Mosiah 6:9 [9:6]). The Lamanites who were already living there were required to leave. Zeniff's people immediately went to work to build up and repair the cities, to begin farming, and to tend their flocks.

After twelve years, the Lamanite King began to fear the growing strength of the Nephites and became increasingly jealous of their abundant crops and flocks. During the following year, the Lamanites attacked and stole some of their crops and livestock. The Nephites successfully drove the Lamanites out of their land and fortified their cities. There was peace for an additional twenty-two years.

The Lamanite king died *"and his son began to reign in his stead"* (Mosiah 6:34 [10:6]). This new Lamanite king stirred up a rebellion against Zeniff's colony. He led his people into battle but was defeated.

KING NOAH

King Noah's Evil Ways

As time passed, the aging Zeniff conferred the kingdom on his son, Noah. He was a wicked king who followed *"after the desires of his own heart. And he had many wives and concubines"* (Mosiah 7:2–3 [11:2]). Noah also imposed a heavy tax on his own people.

> *And it came to pass that he placed his heart upon his riches, and he spent his time in riotous living with his wives and his concubines; and so did also his priests spend their time with harlots. And it came to pass that he planted vineyards round about in the land; and he built wine presses, and made wine in abundance; and therefore he became a wine bibber, and also his people.*
>
> —Mosiah 7:20–21 (11:14–15)

During Noah's reign, the animosities with the Lamanites continued.

> *…the Lamanites began to come in upon his people, upon small numbers, and to slay them in their fields, and while they were tending their flocks. And king Noah sent guards round about the land to keep them off; but he did not send a sufficient number, and the Lamanites came upon them and killed them, and drove many of their flocks out of the*

land: thus the Lamanites began to destroy them and to exercise their hatred upon them.

—Mosiah 7:22–24 (11:16–17)

Noah then sent his armies and for a time they were successful at protecting his people.

Abinadi, the Prophet

The Lord told the prophet, Abinadi, to warn King Noah and his priests that they needed to repent or else! He confronted them with his scriptural knowledge and accused them of being hypocrites. King Noah had him burned to death. However, during Abinadi's speech before Noah and his court, a priest of Noah, Alma, understood and believed what Abinadi was saying. When Alma tried to speak up, he was threatened with death. He quickly escaped and went into hiding.

Alma's Escape to Zarahemla

Alma wrote down what Abinadi had said and began to secretly teach some of the people. He soon took his followers to a place near the edge of the wilderness and built up a church. Eventually, King Noah's spies discovered Alma and his people. They had to make a quick retreat eight days further into the wilderness. There they lived and prospered for a period of time. Ultimately, they were discovered again, this time by the Lamanites. They were enslaved and subjected to heavy burdens. Alma's people prayed to the Lord while seeking a means to escape.

On a night designated by the Lord, "*the Lord caused a deep sleep to come upon the Lamanites…*" (Mosiah 11:68 [24:119]). During that night, the people quickly departed into the wilderness. When they paused in a valley to praise the Lord, they were told to leave the valley and the Lord would stop their pursuers in that valley. A heavy rain upstream could have easily produced a temporary flood that would have blocked their pursuers.

Alma and his followers were probably following the headwaters of the Usumacinta River down to the lowlands. The Usumacinta River flows past Yaxchilan.

> *And it came to pass that they departed out of the valley, and took their journey into the wilderness. And it came to pass that after they had been in the wilderness twelve days, they arrived to the land of Zarahemla; and king Mosiah did also receive them with joy*
>
> —Mosiah 11:75–76 (24:24–25)

Their arrival probably occurred shortly after King Benjamin, designated his son, Mosiah, the younger, to be the new Nephite king. This Mosiah was the grandson of Mosiah, the elder, who had sent Zeniff back to Lamanite territory many years earlier.

End of King Noah's Reign

Meanwhile, the continuing wickedness of King Noah caused his people to rebel against him. They were about to kill him when the Lamanite army suddenly invaded. King Noah told the people to flee. King Noah even told the men to save themselves and to abandon their wives and children. Many were killed and many surrendered. King Noah escaped; however, his people were so angry with him that they *"caused that he should suffer, even unto death by fire"* (Mosiah 9:96 [19:20]). Noah's appointed priests fled into the wilderness. The remaining survivors surrendered and were forced to become subservient to the demands of the Lamanite leaders.

DESPERATION OF KING LIMHI

King Limhi

Limhi, grandson of Zeniff, became a puppet king of this now-conquered kingdom. The Lamanites placed guards around them to make sure that they did not try to escape. Limhi tried to reign in peace.

The Lamanites placed a heavy tax on the population. This tribute was in the amount of:

> *one half of all they possessed; one half of their gold, and their silver, and all their precious things; and thus they should pay tribute to the king of the Lamanites, from year to year*

> —Mosiah 9:90 (19:15).

After the priests of King Noah had been in hiding for two years, an opportunity presented itself. They kidnapped twenty-four daughters of the Lamanites. The people of King Limhi were blamed, which led to a bloody battle between the Lamanites and Limhi's subjects. In the process, the Lamanite king was wounded and captured. He was brought before King Limhi. Limhi asked the Lamanite king why he had attacked his people when they had done no wrong. They soon concluded that it was the priests of Noah who had carried away those daughters.

Although the Lamanites swore an oath to be peaceful, many repeatedly invaded the land of King Limhi. Limhi's people tried going to battle against these invaders but were defeated and many Nephites were killed.

> *And now there was a great mourning and lamentation among the people of Limhi; the widow mourning for her husband; the son and the daughter mourning for their father; and the brothers for their brethren. Now there were a great many widows in the land; and they did cry mightily from day to day, for a great fear of the Lamanites had come upon them.*
>
> —Mosiah 9:148-149 (21:9-10)

Out of revenge, they wanted to attack the Lamanites. King Limhi finally relented. They tried going to battle again—and lost; then a third time—and lost. As a result, greater demands were placed on them by the Lamanites. In their suffering, the Nephites began to repent. King Limhi commanded his people to support the widows and fatherless children. They had to work together to keep their grain and flocks safe. King Limhi always had his guards with him when he was outside the walls of the city.

King Limhi Sends for Help

In desperation, King Limhi sent forty-three of his people into the wilderness to search for Zarahemla. He was hoping "*that we might appeal unto our brethren to deliver us out of bondage*" (Mosiah 5:60 [8:7]). These forty-three people were the children or grandchildren of that group that came up from Zarahemla under the leadership of Zeniff. None had ever seen Zarahemla or knew the exact route to be taken.

Search Party Discovers Jaredite Remains

The search party must have followed the stream that they thought would lead them to Zarahemla. Many days later, when they returned, they spoke of discovering:

> ...a land which was covered with bones of men, and of beasts...and was also covered with ruins of buildings of every kind; And for a testimony that the things that they have said is true, they have brought twenty-four plates, which are filled with engravings; and they are of pure gold. And behold, also, they have brought breast-plates, which are large; and they are of brass, and of copper, and are perfectly sound.
>
> —Mosiah 5:62–65 (8:8–10)

As a result, the search party believed everyone in Zarahemla had died and no help would ever be found. The combined burden of the persecution and enslavement by the Lamanites and the lost hope of rescue must have been very depressing.

When searching for Zarahemla, the search party mistakenly found a remnant of the Jaredite carnage. Recall, from the story of the Jaredites:

> —And so great...had been the war, and so long had been the scene of bloodshed and carnage, that the whole face of the land was covered with the bodies of the dead; and so swift and speedy was the war, that there was none left to bury the dead...
>
> —Ether 6:57–58 (14:21–22)

How did this search party get so lost? The part of the land of Nephi where they started their journey must have been between the headwaters of two major river systems. They had been living there for two generations. All they knew was to follow a stream through the forests and rugged terrain to Zarahemla. However, there was no memory among them to know which stream to follow. During all those years, it is also possible for a simple mudslide or avalanche to easily alter the route of a small stream.

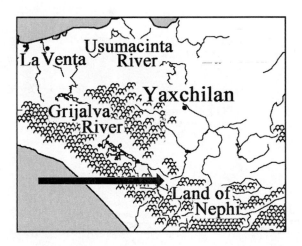

Instead of following the headwaters of the Usumacinta River (River Sidon) downstream to Yaxchilan (city of Zarahemla), they followed the headwaters of the Grijalva River by mistake. This route would have taken them further west and into the Jaredite territory.

La Venta is on the Tonalá River. The headwaters of the Tonalá River are close to the Grijalva River. La Venta (the Jaredite land of Moron) was where the Jaredite Ether had warned Coriantumr to repent. After he was threatened, Ether escaped by hiding "*in the cavity of a rock*" (Ether 6:14–15 [13:13–14]).

Ether's *"cavity of a rock"* or cave was probably near the headwaters of the Tonalá River. That would place it closer to the Grijalva River. Ether had long since passed away before Limhi's search party arrived, but he had left behind a record of his people on twenty-four gold plates.

Limhi's search party may have encountered a thunderstorm and quickly took shelter in an available cave. By the Lord's design, it may have been the same one that had sheltered Ether and that is where they found the plates. The search party could not appreciate what was written on them since they had no way to translate the strange engravings. However, they felt as though they had to show King Limhi this unusual treasure.

MISSION SENT FROM ZARAHEMLA

King Mosiah Sends Ammon

At the time that Alma and his followers had escaped, King Noah was still ruling the people in wickedness. Alma had taken with him the records of Zeniff and his record of Abinadi's warnings to King Noah and his priests. After Alma's arrival in Zarahemla, Mosiah called the people together to read to them the records of Zeniff.

After a period of peace, Mosiah and others became curious and wondered what had happened to the people under King Noah. After King Mosiah had been on the throne for three years, he sent Ammon and fifteen other men to the land of Nephi to investigate (Mosiah 5:1–3 [7:1–2]). Also during that same third year of his reign, Mosiah's father, King Benjamin passed away (Mosiah 4:7 [6:5]). Since the death of King Benjamin and the departure of Ammon and his men appear to have occurred during the same third year, Ammon's departure may have preceded King Benjamin's death.

It took Ammon forty days to go up to the land of Lehi-Nephi (Mosiah 5:6 [7:5]). Ammon and his men were probably following the Usumacinta River (River Sidon) upstream. It had been years before anyone had traveled to the highlands. The search party finally emerged from the wilderness north of the land of Shilom. Ammon took three men with him to go down into the land of Nephi.

King Limhi Meets Ammon

> ...and behold, they met the king of the people, which was in the land of Nephi, and in the land of Shilom; and they were surrounded by the king's guard, and was taken, and was bound, and was committed to prison.
>
> —Mosiah 5:8–9 (7:7)

Recall that for his safety and the safety of his people, King Limhi had posted guards around the city. As Ammon and his men approached, the assumption was made that these were some of Noah's priests.

Interestingly, Ammon and his men were quickly recognized as Nephites. As will be discussed in a later chapter, the Mayans (Lamanites) had a custom of tattooing their faces and upper body. Apparently, the Nephites never adopted this practice. It is likely that the lack of tattoos quickly identified them as Nephites. The people of Limhi believed that everyone in Zarahemla had all died. The only other Nephites they knew about were Noah's priests.

After spending two days in prison, Ammon and those men who were with him were brought before King Limhi. Limhi told them who he was and emphasized his authority over them. He then asked them to explain themselves. Ammon then bowed before the king and said:

For I am Ammon, and am a descendant of Zarahemla,
and have come up out of the land of Zarahemla, to inquire
concerning our brethren, which Zeniff brought up out of
that land…after Limhi had heard the words of Ammon,
he was exceeding glad, and said, Now, I know of a surety
that my brethren…are yet alive.

—Mosiah 5:17–18 (7:13–14)

It is difficult to imagine the joy the people must have felt upon hearing that the people of Zarahemla were alive and the hope of being rescued was restored! The rest of Ammon's search party was brought into the city and all the people must have celebrated.

King Benjamin or King Mosiah?

When Ammon was shown the plates of ore that Limhi's search party had found:

…Limhi was again filled with joy, on learning from the
mouth of Ammon that king Benjamin had a gift from
God, whereby he could interpret such engravings; yea, and
Ammon also did rejoice.

—Mosiah 9:170 (21:28)

It was King Mosiah who had sent these men on this mission, and it would be King Mosiah who would ultimately provide a translation of these engravings. However, if Ammon departed Zarahemla before King Benjamin's death, he may have naturally associated King Benjamin with the use of the interpreters—an instrument provided by the Lord for translating languages.[70]   It was later thought that a translation error had occurred. The quote above is from the 1830 edition of the Book of Mormon. Believing it to be an error, some subsequent editions of the Book of Mormon have changed it to read, "*king Mosiah had a gift....*" It may have been an honest mistake on the part of Ammon. When Mormon wrote his abridgment of this part of the record, this honest mistake was continued.[71]

If King Benjamin passed away shortly after Ammon's departure from Zarahemla, it would place the timing of these events at around 121 B.C.

King Limhi and His People Escape

King Limhi gathered his people together to determine a means of escape. A man named Gideon provided the answer.

> *And Gideon saith unto him, Behold the back pass through the back wall, on the back side of the city. The Lamanites, or the guards of the Lamanites, by night, are drunken; therefore let us send a proclamation among all this people, that they gather together their flocks and herds, that they may drive them into the wilderness by night.*
>
> —Mosiah 10:8–9 (22:5–6)

On the designated day that they chose to escape:

> *...king Limhi caused that his people should gather their flocks together; and he sent the tribute of wine to the*

---

70   More information will be provided regarding the interpreters in Chapter 10: Moroni, Those Plates, and His Journey.

71   More will be said regarding the possession of the interpreters in Chapter 10, Moroni, Those Plates, and His Journey.

Lamanites; and he also sent more wine, as a present unto
them: and they did drink freely of the wine which king
Limhi did send unto them.

—Mosiah 10:13 (22:10)

Limhi's people left that night through that secret pass. The guards were drunk and asleep. They traveled around the land of Shilom and into the wilderness. Ammon and his men knew which stream to follow.

When the Lamanites discovered the people missing, they sent an army to bring them back. However, after two days, the army was no longer able to follow them.

Upon the arrival of Ammon and the people of Limhi in the land of Zarahemla:

Mosiah received them with joy; and he also received their
records, and also the records which had been found by the
people of Limhi.

—Mosiah 10:17 (22:14)

The people of King Limhi then became subjects of King Mosiah, the younger.

GEOGRAPHY BASED TRAVEL TIMES

The travel times of people between Zarahemla and the land of Lehi-Nephi are interesting and supportive of this proposed geography. The following is a review of the sequence of events with a focus on those travel times.

Initially, Zeniff had migrated down to Zarahemla with King Mosiah I, and then returned to the land of Lehi-Nephi in an unsuccessful attempt to spy on the Lamanites. He returned to Zarahemla. However, he then described this second trip from Zarahemla to the land of Lehi-Nephi as taking "*many days wandering in the wilderness*" (Mosiah 6:6–7 [9:3–4]). Along the way, they suffered from many difficulties which he blamed on their being "...*slow to remember the Lord our God*" (Mosiah 6:6 [9:3]). If the path had been easy to follow, his second journey to the land of Lehi-Nephi should have been simple.

A generation later, Alma would lead a group of followers back to Zarahemla. He had converted many people to Christ through his preaching. However, he had to hide from King Noah and his men in the process. For their safety, they had been camping "...*in the borders of the land...*" of Lehi-Nephi (Mosiah 9:68 [18:31]). After their location was discovered, the Lord warned Alma and "*they...departed into the wilderness. And they were in number about four hundred and fifty souls*" (Mosiah 9:72–73 [18:34–35]). Their new camp was eight days further into the wilderness (Mosiah 11:3 [23:3]). They had settled in this new location for a time and even built a city. Nevertheless, they were eventually discovered by a Lamanite army and, for a time, were forced to live in captivity. However, their faith in the Lord was rewarded. On a designated night, they quietly escaped, and twelve days later they were in Zarahemla! Counting the eight days to the place where they built a city plus twelve days in the wilderness to reach Zarahemla would mean that their journey lasted only twenty days. This involved at least 450 people and their flocks!

Sometime after Alma's arrival in Zarahemla, the people were curious regarding the remaining descendants of Zeniff's colony. King Mosiah sent sixteen men to investigate. Those sixteen men "*wandered many days in the wilderness, even forty days...*" (Mosiah 5:3–5 [7:2–4]).

Sixteen men took forty days to go up to the land of Lehi-Nephi from Zarahemla. Compare that with 450 people with their flocks taking twenty days to go the same distance from the other direction. Also, consider the fact that none of those traveling down to Zarahemla ever got lost, except for that one search party that followed the wrong stream. This supports the idea that they navigated through the mountainous tropical forest by simply following the Usumacinta River or one of its tributaries. When traveling downstream, one need only follow the stream's flow. However, when traveling upstream, various tributaries would be encountered. Each time, a choice had to be made regarding which one to follow. Since many tributaries flow into the Usumacinta River, an occasional wrong choice would be expected. The result would be getting lost, backtracking, and wandering more days in the wilderness.

It is also interesting to note that there are multiple references to people going *"up to the land of Lehi-Nephi"* (Mosiah 5:3, 5 [7:2, 4]) or *"up to the land of Nephi"* (Mosiah 9:114; 12:1, 9; 13:5 [20:7; 28:1, 5; 29:3]). "Up" is a reference to a change in elevation.

ABOUT THOSE PLATES OF GOLD

The twenty-four gold plates discovered by Limhi's search party were now in the hands of Mosiah II in the city of Zarahemla. It was Ether's record of the history of his people. It is from those twenty-four gold plates that, many years later, Moroni would write an abridgment of the history of the Jaredites. That summary became what is called the Book of Ether.

CONCLUSION

Events described in the Book of Mormon combined with some geography provide us with one compatible account. Credible geography helps us understand how that search party got so lost. There is also support for understanding how people navigated through the rugged mountainous terrain between the city of Zarahemla and the land of Lehi-Nephi by simply following a stream. Taken together, all of this complements and supports the belief that these were...

REAL PEOPLE IN REAL PLACES!

CHAPTER 6:

LAMONI AND THE LAND OF JERSHON

Introduction

With the help of the Lord, the missionary sons of Mosiah II were instrumental in the conversion of several thousand Lamanites. The focus of this chapter is to appreciate the size of the population that moved from the land of Nephi to the land of Jershon. In the end, it will provide some idea of the geography of these ancient peoples.

LAMANITES CONVERTED TO THE LORD

Sons of Mosiah in the Land of Nephi

Mosiah II had been king for many years. Upon his death, there were to be no more kings. This was out of fear that an unrighteous ruler might come to power. Besides, the sons of Mosiah did not want to become king. Upon his death, the people were to be ruled by a group of judges that would be elected by the people.

Mosiah died "*five hundred and nine years from the time Lehi left Jerusalem*" (Mosiah 13:67 [29:46]) or about 91 B.C.[72] During this

---

72   This is based on "Book of Mormon years" which will be discussed at length in Chapter 9.

same year, the sons of Mosiah were full of the Spirit and anxious to be missionaries among the Lamanites. The sons of Mosiah:

...departed out of the land of Zarahemla [Yaxchilan], *and took their swords, and their spears, and their bows, and their arrows, and their slings...that they might provide food for themselves while in the wilderness: and thus they departed into the wilderness, with their numbers which they had selected, to go up to the land of Nephi, to preach the word of God unto the Lamanites. ...they journeyed many days in the wilderness, and they fasted much, and prayed much, that the Lord would grant unto them a portion of his spirit to go with them, and abide with them, that they might be an instrument in the hands of God, to bring, if it were possible, their brethren, the Lamanites, to the knowledge of the truth*

—Alma 12:11–15 (17:7–9)

The spirit of the Lord comforted them along the way.

After they arrived in the land of Nephi, *"Ammon went* [alone] *to the land of Ishmael"* (Alma 12:29 [17:19]) in the land of Nephi. He was quickly captured by the Lamanites. They bound him and took him before their king, King Lamoni. It was the king's choice whether to have this Nephite invader killed, imprisoned, enslaved or cast out of his land (Alma 12:31 [17:20]).

When Ammon stood before the king, he told him that he wanted to remain among *"this people...perhaps until the day I die"* (Alma 12:34 [17:23]). Upon his request to become a servant to the king, he was assigned to help watch over the king's flocks.

On one occasion, while the king's flocks were being watered, seven men scattered the flocks. The king's servants were very afraid of losing the king's flocks. If lost, they knew they would all be sentenced to death. Ammon quickly comforted them and helped them gather the flocks. When the same men tried a second time to scatter them, Ammon single-handedly defended the flocks. The other servants kept the flocks safe and witnessed the confrontation. They marveled that Ammon was able to defeat so many thieves without help and without being wounded in the process. These servants began to think of him as more than a mortal man. They told the king and many other people of this seemingly miraculous feat. All were amazed at his faithfulness and his power.

King Lamoni and His People are Converted

After King Lamoni heard of Ammon's feat, he called Ammon before him. The king silently wondered what kind of man he was. Ammon then spoke up.

> *I say unto you, what is it, that thy marvellings are so great? Behold, I am a man, and am thy servant; therefore, whatsoever thou desirest which is right, that will I do. Now when the king had heard these words, he marvelled again, for he beheld that Ammon could discern his thoughts; but notwithstanding this, king Lamoni...said unto him, Who art thou? Art thou that Great Spirit, which knows all things? Ammon answered and said unto him, I am not.*

> —Alma 12:90–94 (18:17–19)

King Lamoni permitted Ammon to continue speaking. Missionary-minded Ammon began to explain that the Great Spirit that

King Lamoni believed in is God. He talked about God, His angels, heaven, creation, and all the scriptures. He also spoke of the rebellious Laman, Lemuel, and Ishmael.

> *…after he* [Ammon] *said all these things, and expounded them to the king, that the king believed all his words. And he began to cry unto the Lord, saying: O Lord, have mercy…upon me and my people.*
>
> —Alma 12:121–122 (18:40–41)

What followed was a miraculous conversion of King Lamoni and his household (Alma 12:142–170 [19:12–29]).

As King Lamoni and his wife recovered from their powerful spiritual experience, people began to contend with each other over the meaning of it all. King Lamoni began to scold them. The King and his servants declared to the people that "*their hearts had been changed; that they had no more desire to do evil*" (Alma 12:176 [19:33]). Many claimed that they saw angels and spoke with them. As a result, many believed and were baptized. A church was soon established among the people of King Lamoni.

After a church was established, King Lamoni wanted Ammon to go with him to visit his father, who was the king over the whole land. However, the Lord told Ammon that Lamoni's father would try to kill him. Instead, he was to go to Middoni to rescue his brother, Aaron, and two companions. King Lamoni told him that he would go with him since the king of Middoni was a good friend. Lamoni was sure that he could flatter the king into releasing those prisoners.

While en route to Middoni, they encountered Lamoni's father, who considered all Nephites to be enemies. He saw his son defending this Nephite and traveling to have other Nephites released from prison. Lamoni's father drew his sword to kill Ammon. Ammon defended himself by disabling the king. The king pleaded for his life and promised that his son, Lamoni, could retain his kingdom and that Ammon's brothers would be released from prison.

Lamoni's Father and His People are Converted

After their rescue, Aaron and his companions went to see Lamoni's father, the king over the whole land. They bowed before him, introduced themselves, and said they wanted to be his servants. This approach allowed Aaron to bear his testimony to the King regarding all the scriptures, beginning with Adam and the fall of man to the plan of redemption through Christ. A miraculous conversion experience of King Lamoni's father followed. He, in turn, converted his whole household (Alma 13:33–64 [22:3–23]).

The Lamanite king then sent out a proclamation that Ammon, Aaron, and their companions were not to be harmed. They were to be allowed to preach the word of God wherever they chose (Alma 14:1 [23:1]). The king's goal was that:

> ...his people might be convinced concerning the wicked traditions of their fathers, and that they might be convinced that they were all brethren, and that they had not ought to murder, nor to plunder, nor to steal, nor to commit adultery, not to commit any manner of wickedness.
>
> —Alma 14:5–6 (23:3)

The Lamanites from several cities were all converted and laid down their weapons of war.

The people wanted to be called by another name besides Lamanites, so they chose to be called Anti-Nephi-Lehies (Alma 14:19 [23:17]). Lamoni's father conferred the kingdom upon Lamoni's brother, who changed his name to Anti-Nephi-Lehi. And their father passed away.

This odd name, Anti-Nephi-Lehi, has been an enigma. It may be a reference to taking a position in opposition to those who had not been converted to the Lord while living in the land of Lehi-Nephi. There is also another possibility.

> ...*if the name element Anti- derives from the Egyptian relative adjective nty, which means "the one who," "that," or "which," then the name would mean just the opposite; roughly, "that-which(-is-of-)Nephi-Lehi" or "the-one-who (-is-of-) Nephi-Lehi."*[73]

In either case, they were declaring to everyone that they were taking on a new identity.

MARTYRDOM OF CONVERTS

Refuse to Take Up Weapons

Many Lamanites who had chosen not to accept the Nephites' words were in a state of rebellion and began to prepare for war. Ammon, Aaron, and their companions spoke to both kings.

---

73   Stephen D. Ricks and Dennis L. Largey, Editor. "Anti-Nephi-Lehi." *Book of Mormon Reference Companion.* Salt Lake City, UT: Deseret Book Company. 2003. p. 67

Now there was not one soul among all the people which had been converted unto the Lord, that would take up arms against their brethren.

—Alma 14:27 (24:6)

The people had repented of the many murders that they had committed in the past and felt forgiven. They had already taken their swords and buried them deep in the earth. They would rather suffer and die than commit sin.

When the Lamanites invaded their land to kill them, "*they went out to meet them, and prostrated themselves before them…and began to call on the name of the Lord*" (Alma 14:49 [24:21]). The Lamanites began to slay them and killed over 1,000 people.

…now when the Lamanites saw this, they did forbear from slaying them; and there were many whose hearts had swollen in them for those of their brethren who had fallen under the sword, for they repented of the things which they had done.…they threw down their weapons of war, and they would not take them again, for they were stung for the murders which they had committed…the people of God were joined that day by more than the number which had been slain.

—Alma 14:51–54 (24:23–26)

Those Lamanites who were not converted to the Lord returned home very angry. They still wanted to slaughter the people of Anti-Nephi-Lehi. Meanwhile, the people of God still refused to take up arms in their defense.

SURVIVORS ESCAPE

Escape to Zarahemla

When Ammon saw that the people would not defend themselves, he suggested to the king, "*let us go down to the land of Zarahemla…and flee out of the hands of our enemies, that we be not destroyed*" (Alma 15:6 [27:5]). However, the king told Ammon that he was afraid that the Nephites would kill them because of their history of "*many murders and sins we have committed against them*" (Alma 15:7 [27:6]). Ammon said he would ask the Lord. The king promised to abide by whatever the Lord had to say.

> *And it came to pass that Ammon went and inquired of the Lord, and the Lord said unto him, Get this people out of this land, that they perish not, for Satan hath great hold on* [them], *which do stir up the Lamanites to anger against their brethren…and blessed art this people in this generation; for I will preserve them.*
>
> —Alma 15:12 (27:11–12)

Ammon shared with the king what the Lord had said. As a result, they gathered the people together, along with their flocks and herds. Ammon, Aaron, and their companions led the people downstream to the land of Zarahemla. From the context of this story, this would have included several thousand people.

As they approached the borders, Ammon told them to wait there while he and his brothers went to talk to the Nephites and to determine their ability to receive this very large migration of Lamanites. In turn, the Chief Judge of the Nephites asked the people if they were willing to admit and accept the people of Anti-Nephi-Lehi.

> *...the voice of the people came saying, Behold, we will give up the land of Jershon, which is on the east by the sea, which joins the land Bountiful, which is on the south of the land of Bountiful; and this land Jershon is the land which we will give unto our brethren, for an inheritance.*
>
> —Alma 15:23 (27:22)

The Book of Mormon makes multiple references to a land called Bountiful.

> According to Ixtlilxóchitl, the name *for "the seat of the kingdom" as of 132 B.C. was Huehuetlapallan, which means "ancient Bountiful land." Hue-hue is from the Nahua (Mexican) tongue and means "old, old" or "ancient." Tlapallan (Tula-pallan) is derived from the primary Maya root Tul, meaning "bountiful or abundance."*[74]

Lamanai = Lamoni

The Mayan names of most cities have been lost to time. However, there is one exception that is of particular interest—Lamanai. It is located in the lowlands, as would be expected for a Nephite city. Ancient Hebrew writing consisted only of consonants and no vowels. Consequently, both Lamanai and Lamoni would be spelled the same—Lmn.

---

74 Milton R. Hunter and Thomas Stuart Ferguson. *Ancient America and the Book of Mormon*. Whitefish, MT: Literary Licensing LLC, 1950. pp. 149–150.

Within the context of this account from the Book of Mormon, it is possible that, when given the land of Jershon, King Lamoni received an already existing city next to a river where his people could live peacefully. As the leader who established his people in this area, the city would have been named after him—Lamoni.

We are told that the land of Jershon was *"on the east by the sea"* (Alma 15:23 [27:22]). From the shore, that land probably extended a short distance inland. Lamanai is one of several archaeological sites in the northern half of Belize and is located less than thirty miles from the eastern side of the Yucatan Peninsula. Lamanai (or the ancient city of Lamoni) could have easily been a part of the land of Jershon. Next to Lamanai is the New River—a crocodile-infested river! The name Lamanai eventually came to mean "submerged crocodile."

The site, known as Lamanai, had been previously occupied.

*Lamanai has one of the longest histories of all the Mayan
sites. It was continuously occupied from around 500 BC…
until 1675 or perhaps even later.*[75]

However, "*…around 100 B.C., a major transformation of the site
took place.*"[76] The timing of this "transformation" corresponds well
with the introduction of the people of Anti-Lehi-Nephi as described in
the Book of Mormon.

The people of Anti-Lehi-Nephi had taken an oath that they
would never take up arms. This oath was honored by the Nephites
when they placed their army between the land of Jershon and the land
of Nephi. This was done to protect them from their Lamanite enemies.
In turn, the people of Anti-Lehi-Nephi were asked to pay a tribute to
the Nephites so they could maintain those armies. After settling in the
land of Jershon, they were given a new name.

*…they were called by the Nephites the people of Ammon;
therefore they were distinguished by that name ever after;
and they were among the people of Nephi, and also numbered among the people which were of the Church of God.*

—Alma 15:29–30 (27:26–27)

---

75   "Lamanai Belize." *Mayan Ruins.* <http://mayanruins.info/belize/lamanai-belize/> 26
       Sep 2019.

76   "What Do We Know about Lamanai?" *Lamanai Archaeology Project.* <https://lamanai.
       org.uk/index.html> 26 Sep 2019.

CONCLUSION

Stories from the Book of Mormon combined with Mayan archaeology and geography provide us with one compatible narrative. Taken together, all of this complements and supports the story of King Lamoni and the land of Jershon as told in the Book of Mormon. I believe these were...

REAL PEOPLE IN REAL PLACES!

CHAPTER 7:

A SKIN OF BLACKNESS

Introduction

I have encountered many misconceptions and even anger regarding the Book of Mormon referring to a "skin of blackness" (2 Nephi 4:35 [5:21]). It is described as a curse placed on the Lamanites by God. As a result, some have suggested that the Book of Mormon and believers of the Book of Mormon are racist. I have also seen people who have used the Book of Mormon to defend their prejudicial attitudes.

Such viewpoints take away from the truth of what happened while, at the same time, portraying a diminished love of God for all people. God created everyone and loves all people equally. The interpretation and understanding of these verses in the Book of Mormon need to be clarified by putting them into the context of the culture and time when it was written.

UNDERSTANDING SCRIPTURES

Original Lamanite Curse

The following is an often-quoted verse from the Book of Mormon.

Thus the word of God is fulfilled, for these are the words which he saith to Nephi: Behold, the Lamanites have I cursed; and I will set a mark upon them, that they and

*their seed may be separated from thee and thy seed, from
this time henceforth and forever, except they repent....
And again: I will set a mark upon him that mingleth his
seed with thy brethren, that they may be cursed also. And
again: I will set a mark upon them that fighteth against
thee and thy seed. And again I say, He that departeth from
thee, shall no more be called thy seed; and I will bless thee,
&c....*

—Alma 1:112–116 (3:14–17)

Notice the "&c" in the verse above. It appears that there was more to this curse than what was written here. Mormon did not copy the whole curse at this point since he apparently quoted the entire curse earlier in his writings. Mormon must have then assumed that whoever had possession of this part of his record would also have the earlier part. Rather than waste space on his precious metal plates, Mormon simply quoted the beginning of the curse and added "&c."[77]

Mormon wrote that these are the words of Nephi. However, this quoted material is not found anywhere in the writings of Nephi.

In 1828, Joseph Smith was busy with the translation of the Book of Mormon. As he would read the translation provided to him by the Lord, his scribe, Martin Harris, would write it down. During this time, Martin pleaded with Joseph Smith that he might borrow the translation to show to others. After translating about one-fourth of the plates and against the advice of the Lord, Joseph did loan it to him. Martin then lost that portion of the translation (or it was stolen). The Lord

---

77   This quote is from the 1830 edition. The "&c." is also found in the 1907 LDS edition and the 1908 RLDS edition. However, many subsequent editions of the Book of Mormon have deleted the "&c."

admonished Joseph and told him that the lost portion was not to be retranslated. That lost portion probably contained the complete text of the curse. Therefore, **the complete text of the curse was lost and is not found anywhere in the Book of Mormon.**

Shortly after Lehi and his family had departed Jerusalem, Nephi's older brothers, Laman and Lemuel, "murmured" against their father, Lehi. Nephi had prayed to the Lord regarding the difficulties between his brothers and his father (1 Nephi 1:38–41 [2:11–12]). The Lord comforted Nephi and made known to him that Lehi was speaking the truth. Nephi made an unsuccessful attempt to convince his older brothers of the errors of their ways. Nephi was left grieving in his heart (1 Nephi 1:47–53 [2:16–19]). The Lord told Nephi:

> ...*inasmuch as thy brethren shall rebel against thee, they shall be cut off from the presence of the Lord. And inasmuch as thou shalt keep my commandments, thou shalt be made a ruler and a teacher over thy brethren. For behold, in that day that they shall rebel against me, I will curse them even with a sore curse, and they shall have no power over thy seed, except they shall rebel against me also. And if it so be that they rebel against me, they shall be a scourge unto thy seed, to stir them up in the ways of remembrance.*
>
> —1 Nephi 1:55–58 (2:21–24)

This is the earliest reference to a pending curse against Laman, Lemuel, and their descendants. It would be based on their rebellion against the Lord. The curse was defined as being "*cut off from the presence of the Lord.*" It had nothing to do with the color of their skin. Notice the following verses:

- *yea, he [Lehi] feared lest they [Laman and Lemuel] should be cast off from the presence of the Lord...* (1 Nephi 2:87 [8:36])

- *for the Lord God hath said, That inasmuch as ye shall keep my commandments, ye shall prosper in the land; and inasmuch as ye will not keep my commandments, ye shall be cut off from my presence.* (2 Nephi 3:8–9 [4:4])

- *Wherefore, the word of the Lord was fulfilled which he spake unto me, saying: That inasmuch as they will not hearken unto thy words, they shall be cut off from his presence. And behold, they were cut off from his presence.* (2 Nephi 4:31–32 [5:20–20])

- *And I would that all men might be saved. But we read that in that great and last day, there are some which shall be cast out; yea, which shall be cast off from the presence of the Lord...* (Helaman 4:72 [12:25])

Giving God Credit for What People Choose

A scripture written several thousand years ago may be misunderstood when viewed within the context of today's language and culture. For example, there are two conflicting biblical references regarding who hardened Pharaoh's heart during the time of Moses.

- *But the Lord hardened the heart of Pharaoh, and he would not listen to them, just as the Lord had spoken to Moses.*[78] (Exo. 9:12, NRSV)

- *Why should you harden your hearts as the Egyptians and Pharaoh hardened their hearts...?* (1 Sam. 6:6, NRSV)

The Lord gave all people the ability to choose to do that which is right or to do that which is contrary to His will. According to 1

---

78   This same verse in Joseph Smith's translation of the Bible (Inspired Version) reads: "*And Pharaoh hardened his heart, and he hearkened not unto them...*"

Samuel, the Lord permitted the Egyptians and Pharoah, using their agency, to harden their own hearts. The verse from Exodus appears to give God credit for something that Pharoah did to himself. God would not intentionally harden a person's heart so that he or she would have a desire to violate His will.

> *For behold, they had hardened their hearts against him, that they had become like unto a flint; wherefore, as they were white, and exceeding fair and delightsome, that they might not be enticing unto my people, therefore the Lord God did cause a skin of blackness to come upon them.*
>
> —2 Nephi 4:34–35 (5:21)

That "skin of blackness" must be understood within the context of the ancient Hebrew culture. In the example above from Exodus, God is given credit for what Pharoah did to himself. Within that same context in the Book of Mormon, God is given credit for what the Lamanites did to themselves. The Lamanites caused a skin of blackness to come upon themselves as an outward display of their rebellion against the Lord and His people.

Many years later, during a continuing war with the Lamanites, it was noted that:

> *...the skins of the Lamanites were dark, according to the mark which was set upon their fathers, which was a curse upon them because of their transgression and their rebellion against their brethren, which consisted of Nephi, Jacob, and Joseph, and Sam, which were just and holy men.*
>
> —Alma 1:104 (3:6)

Again, the curse is related to their rebellion against God and His people. It had nothing to do with the color of their skin.

TATTOOS AND PAINTED SKIN

Egyptian Tattoos

Egyptian artwork and many Egyptian mummies show evidence of tattoos—depicting mostly abstract designs.

> *Several mummies have been recovered that date to as early as the XI Dynasty (2160–1994 B.C.) that exhibit tattoo art forms… Beyond the geometric designs that were favoured, other designs discovered were found that were intrinsically connected to religion. Mummies dating from roughly 1300 BC are tattooed with pictographs symbolizing Neith, a prominent female deity with a militaristic bent. These are the only tattoos that at this point seem to have a link with male bearers.*[79]

At the time that Lehi left Jerusalem, the Egyptians had been practicing the art of tattooing for many centuries. Lehi and his family were very familiar with Egyptian culture. The older rebellious brothers, Laman and Lemuel, had probably visited Egypt on many occasions with their father. As such, they would have been well aware of the Egyptian practice of tattooing.

Tattoos were forbidden by Jewish law: "*You shall not make any gashes in your flesh for the dead or tattoo any marks upon you: I am*

---

79   "Ancient Egypt." *The World's Largest Online Tattoo Museum.* <http://www.vanishing-tattoo.com/tattoo_museum/egyptian_tattoos.html> 28 Sep 2019.

the Lord" (Lev. 19:28, NRSV). However, Jehoiakim was the king of Judah for nearly a decade before Lehi left Jerusalem. "...*Jehoiakim as a godless tyrant...had tattooed his body.*[80] As a part of their rebellion, Laman and Lemuel may have followed Jehoiakim's example. They may have shared his rebellious attitude by marking themselves with tattoos. They would have then encouraged tattooing among their descendants.

Mayan Tattoos

> *Mayans practiced many forms of body modification, including deforming a baby's skull...filing teeth, inlaying jade into a tooth, piercing. and tattooing. The Mayans did this to be pleasing to their gods, for social status and for personal beauty...Both Mayan men and women got tattoos, although men put off getting tattoos until they were married. Mayan women preferred delicate tattoos on their upper bodies although not on their breasts. Men got tattoos on their arms, legs, backs, hands, and face.*[81]

Recall from an earlier chapter, the story was told of Ammon being sent by King Mosiah to investigate the remnants of Zeniff's colony. When King Limhi's guards saw Ammon, they immediately knew that this stranger was a Nephite. It is suggested here that Ammon's lack of tattoos was the key that allowed those guards to quickly identify him as such.

---

80 Emil G. Hirsch, et al. "Jehoiakim." *Jewish Encyclopedia.* 1906. <http://www.jewishen-cyclopedia.com/articles/8562-jehoiakim> 28 Dec 2019.

81 Michael Scott Rank, Editor. "Mayan Art of the Tattoo" *History on the Net.* <https://www.historyonthenet.com/mayan-art-of-the-tattoo/> 30 May 2018.

Skin Painted Black

As the aggressors in varying battles with the Nephites, the Lamanites probably wanted to create some form of camouflage. Armies of today often use camouflage so that they can remain undetected until the attack begins. In the jungles of Central America, a good camouflage would be to color one's skin to blend in with the shadows—black paint.

Charles Phillips provides an illustration of a "*Veracruz Figurine c. AD 250–500* [that] *represents a club-wielding warrior with skin blackened for battle.*"[82] And then, from another source, "*Until marriage, young* [Mayan] *men painted themselves black (and so did warriors at all times)…*"[83]

The paint or tattoo could serve to identify a warrior's alliance, camouflage and, during the attack, make him appear more fearsome to the enemy.

The Lamanite's "black skin" became a part of their identity as seen and recorded by the Nephites.

Amlicites Marked Themselves

The Amlicites were a group of Nephites under the leadership of Amlici. They altered their allegiance and joined forces with the Lamanites against their fellow Nephites. In preparation for battle, the Lamanites marked themselves. The Amilicites needed to also mark themselves to prevent confusion with their Nephite enemies during the impending combat.

---

82   Charles Phillips. *The Complete Illustrated History: Aztec & Maya.* NY: Metro Books. 2008. p. 437.

83   Michael D. Coe. *The Maya*, 7th ed. New York: Thames & Hudson. 2005. p. 207.

And the Amlicites were distinguished from the Nephites, for they had marked themselves with red in their foreheads, after the manner of the Lamanites; nevertheless, they had not shorn their heads like unto the Lamanites.

—Alma 1:102 (3:4).

Now the Amlicites knew not that they were fulfilling the words of God when they began to mark themselves in their foreheads; nevertheless, they had come out in open rebellion against God; therefore it was expedient that the curse should fall upon them.—Now I would that ye should see that they brought upon themselves the curse.

—Alma 1:117–119 (3:18–19)

By distinguishing themselves that way, the Amlicites were openly rebelling against God and His people. Notice that the curse was not determined by the color. It was neither the tattooing nor painting the skin that brought the Lord's curse upon them. It was the manifest display of their open rebellion against the Lord and His people that caused the curse to come upon them.

WHITENESS = PURE HEART

In the Book of Mormon

In these Book of Mormon scriptures, white is correlated with righteousness before the Lord.

- *And behold, they are righteous forever; for because of their faith in the Lamb of God, their garments are made white in his blood.* (1 Nephi 3:117 [12:10])

- *O my brethren, I fear, that unless ye shall repent of your sins, that their skins will be whiter than yours when ye shall be brought with them before the throne of God.* (Jacob 2:59 [3:8])

- *O then ye unbelieving, turn ye unto the Lord; cry mightily unto the Father in the name of Jesus, that perhaps ye may be found spotless, pure, fair, and white, having been cleansed by the blood of the Lamb, at that great and last day.* (Mormon 4:65 [9:6])

- *And the Gospel of Jesus Christ shall be declared among them; wherefore, they shall be restored unto the knowledge of their fathers, and also to the knowledge of Jesus Christ, which was had among their fathers. And then shall they rejoice, for they shall know that it is a blessing unto them from the hand of God; and their scales of darkness shall begin to fall from their eyes; and many generations shall not pass away among them, save they shall be a white and a delightsome people.* (2 Nephi 12:82–84 [30:5–6])

The above phrase "a white and a delightsome people" appears in the printer's manuscript of the Book of Mormon. It was then used in the original 1830 Palmyra and 1837 Kirtland editions. The 1840 Nauvoo edition, which included corrections suggested by Joseph Smith, the word "white" was changed to read "pure." However, the early LDS editions through 1920 continued to use the word "white." The 1908 RLDS edition reintroduced the phrase "a white and a delightsome people" based on the original printer's manuscript. In the 1981 LDS edition, it reads "a pure and a delightsome people." "White" is based on the original translation while "pure" is a better representation of the cultural intent.

The statement that "their skins will be whiter" if people repent cannot be taken to literally mean the actual color of a person's skin.

Scriptural references to a person's skin or their garments being white are simply referring to their righteousness as recognized by God.

In the Bible

A similar theme of whiteness associated with purity of heart occurs in the Bible.

- *Let thy garments be always white; and let thy head lack no ointment* (Ecclesiastes 9:8, KJV).

- *…though your sins be as scarlet, they shall be as white as snow; though they be red like crimson, they shall be as wool* (Isaiah 1:18, KJV).

- *Purge me with hyssop, and I shall be clean: wash me, and I shall be whiter than snow* (Psalms 51:7, KJV).

- *Many shall be purified, and made white…* (Daniel 12:10, KJV).

- *…These are they which came out of great tribulation, and have washed their robes, and made them white in the blood of the Lamb* (Revelations 7:14, KJV).

LAMANITE CURSE LIFTED

Around 13 A.D., a group known as the Gadianton robbers killed many people and destroyed entire cities. Some of the Lamanites joined the Nephites to fight against them. As a result:

> "*…those Lamanites which had united with the Nephites were numbered among the Nephites; and their curse was taken from them, and their skin became white like unto the Nephites; and their young men and their daughters became exceeding fair…*"

> —3 Nephi 1:52–53 (2:14–16).

How can the appearance of such a curse be lifted so quickly? By washing off the black war paint or letting it wear off, the skin became fairer. By stopping the tattooing, the visible sign of their rebellion against the Lord would completely disappear in one generation. Notice that specific mention is made here of their "*young men and their daughters became exceeding fair.*"

CONCLUSION

The curse was the result of transgression and open rebellion against God. The punishment was being cut off from the presence of the Lord. Redemption begins with repentance and keeping the Lord's commandments.

God loves all of His creation and is not a respecter of persons. From a different context within the Book of Mormon:

> *…He inviteth them all to come unto him, and partake of his goodness; and he denieth none that come unto him, black and white, bond and free, male and female and he remembereth the heathen, and all alike unto God, both Jew and Gentile.*
>
> —2 Nephi 11:113–115 (26:33)

The "skin of blackness" among the Lamanites was a self-imposed means of identifying their open rebellion against the Lord. When the Nephites saw the Lamanites in battle, their black skin was obvious. The descriptions of the skin of blackness in the Book of Mormon, in the context of their Hebrew culture and writing style, are reflected in the traditions of the ancient Maya. I believe these were all...

REAL PEOPLE IN REAL PLACES!

CHAPTER 8:

CHRIST IN MORMON AND MAYAN HISTORIES

Introduction

The Book of Mormon was published in 1830. Eleven years later, John Lloyd Stephens, an English explorer in Mexico and Central America, published a book.[84] He described multiple sites where ancient remnants of lost cultures had lived. Before that time, the people of North America had no concept of large populations with highly advanced cultures in Mexico and Central America. As time passed, more and more archaeological evidence provided proof of these ancient populations with cities larger than those in ancient Rome.

Trying to understand and appreciate some of the early histories of the Mayans has limitations. Archbishop Diego de Landa was among the early Catholic missionaries. They believed that the Mayan religious practices were of the devil.

For at least a decade, de Landa and the other friars were zealous in trying to convert the Maya people to Catholicism. He organized masses where Maya nobles were ordered to give up their ancient beliefs and to embrace the new religion. He also ordered inquisition trials against those Maya

---

84   John L. Stephens. *Incidents of Travel in Central America, Chiapas, and Yucatan.* NY: Harper & Brothers. 1841.

who refused to renounce to their faith, and many of them were killed.[85]

After hearing of Roman Catholic Maya who continued to practice idol worship, he [Archbishop Diego de Landa] *ordered an Inquisition…ending with a ceremony called auto de fé, during which an unclear number of Maya codices (according to Landa, 27 books) and approximately 5,000 Maya cult images were burned.*[86]

Only a few relics survived. While researching Mayan history, one is confronted with the destruction of many of their records, the death of some of their leaders, and memories influenced by Christian teachings. Any conclusions regarding correlations with the Mayan legends and the Book of Mormon must be done with some caution.

HISTORICAL SOURCES

Fernando de Alva Cortés Ixtlilxóchitl

In 1428, the Aztecs were formed from the alliance of different indigenous groups. Ixtlilxóchitl's ancestors, the Chichimecas, were a part of that alliance. The Chichimecas were considered at one time to have been a *"descendants of nomadic hunter-gatherers."* [87] They had been

85   Nicoletta Maestri. "Diego de Landa (1524–1579), Bishop and Inquisitor of Early Colonial Yucatan." *ThoughtCo.* 8 Mar 2017. <https://www.thoughtco.com/diego-de-landa-inquisitor-colonial-yucatan-171622> 30 Nov 2019.

86   "On This Day in History: Spanish Priest Diego de Landa Burned the Sacred Books of Maya—On July 12, 1562." *Ancient Pages.* Jul 12, 2016. <http://www.ancientpages.com/2016/07/12/on-this-day-in-history-spanish-priest-diego-de-landa-burned-the-sacred-books-of-maya-on-july-12-1562/> 1 Oct 2019.

87   Christopher Muscato. "Historical Chichimeca Peoples: Culture & History." *History, Culture & People of the Americas.* <https://study.com/academy/lesson/historical-chichimeca-peoples-culture-history.html> 1 Oct 2019.

living in the northern part of central Mexico for many centuries. It is interesting to note that they were "*sky worshipping people*"[88] as opposed to the "*idol worshipping culture of central Mexico.*"[89]

> Fernando de Alva Ixtlilxóchitl *was a distinguished student at the Imperial College of Santa Cruz de Tlatelolco, where he was educated in both... [Aztec], and Spanish. In 1608, he was employed as [an] interpreter by the viceroy, which appointment he received due to his learning and skill in explaining the hieroglyphic pictures of the ancient Mexicans. He had also a profound knowledge of the traditions of his ancestors, which were preserved in the national songs, and was friends and well acquainted with several old Indians famous for their knowledge of Mexican history. He was also commissioned by the Spanish viceroy of New Spain to write histories of the indigenous peoples of Mexico. His Relación histórica de la nación tulteca (usually called Relación) was written between 1600 and 1608. This was an account of many events in New Spain* [Mexico], and *many events of the Toltec, ancient pre-Aztec, people.*[90]

Ixtlilxóchitl wrote mostly about the history of his ancestors, the Chichimecas. He described events spanning over several thousand years. He was frequently quoted in the *Popol Vuh* and Bancroft's *Native Races*, Vol. V.

---

88 Ibid.

89 Ibid.

90 "Fernando de Alva Cortés Ixtlilxóchitl." *Archaeological and Historical Evidence.* <http://www.supportingevidences.net/fernando-de-alva-corts-ixtlilx/> 2 Oct 2019.

Ixtlilxóchitl's works were not published in English until 1848 as part of Lord Kingsborough's *Antiquities of Mexico.*[91]

Popol Vuh

The *Popol Vuh* appears to have begun as an oral history of the ancient Quiché Mayans of Guatemala. Eventually:

> ...*it seems first to have been reduced to writing (in characters of the Latin script), in the middle of the sixteenth century...by some unknown but highly educated...member of that race.*[92]

In the early eighteenth century, a Dominican priest, Francisco Ximénez, copied the Mayan text. The original document has since been lost. A copy of the *Popol Vuh* was subsequently found in an old Catholic Cathedral in southern Guatemala. A century later, the *Popol Vuh* was published in Europe in both Spanish and French. It was not fully translated into English until 1950.[93]

When Joseph Smith Jr. was working on the translation of the Book of Mormon, he could not have known of these stories and legends. However, there are interesting parallels between certain portions of the Book of Mormon and the stories described in the *Popol Vuh*. It is understood that some of the reported Mayan legends may have been colored by the Christian teachings of the Catholic missionaries.

---

91   Lord Kingsborough. *Antiquities of Mexico,* Vol. IX. London, Henry G. Bohn, York St., Covent Garden. 1848.

92   T. D. Goetz and S. G. Morley, translators. From the translation of Adrian Recinos. *Popol Vuh, The Sacred Book of the Ancient Quiché Maya.* Norman, OK: University of Oklahoma Press. 1950. p. ix.

93   Ibid.

However, some aspects, not acknowledged in traditional Christian history, complement the stories found in the Book of Mormon.

Hubert Howe Bancroft

While living in California, Hubert Howe Bancroft accumulated a library consisting of many thousands of mainly historical books. In 1868, he retired so that he could devote all his time to research and writing.

Bancroft wrote a series of publications relating to selected native populations. Volume five focused on Mexico and Central American natives.[94] Bancroft's extensive library probably included Lord Kingsborough's *Antiquities of Mexico* which gave him access to some of the writings of Ixtlilxóchitl. Bancroft's book was published in 1883, fifty-three years after the Book of Mormon was first published. His book does make a brief reference to the basic story of the Book of Mormon—neither endorsing nor condemning it.

BIRTH OF CHRIST

A Day of Three Suns

A Lamanite prophet, Samuel, told the Nephites how they would know of the time of Christ's birth.

> *And behold, he [Samuel] saith unto them, Behold, I give unto you a sign: for five years more cometh, and behold, then cometh the son of God to redeem all those who shall believe on his name. And behold, this will I give unto*

---

94   Hubert H. Bancroft. *The Works of Hubert Howe Bancroft*, Vol. V, *The Native Races, Primitive History.* San Francisco, CA: A. L. Bancroft & Co., Publishers. 1883.

you for a sign at the time of his coming; for behold, there shall be great lights in Heaven, insomuch that in the night before he cometh, there shall be no darkness, insomuch that it shall appear unto man as it is day; therefore there shall be one day and a night, and a day, as if it were one day, and there were no night…for ye shall know of the rising of the sun, and also of its setting…nevertheless the night shall not be darkened; and it shall be night before he is born.

—Helaman 5:55–58 (14:2–4)

Five years after Samuel had delivered that prophecy, some people were claiming that the prophecy was false.

… Now it came to pass that there was a day set apart by the unbelievers, that all those who believed in those traditions [Samuel's prophecies], *should be put to death, except the sign should come to pass…. Now…when Nephi, the son of Nephi, saw the wickedness of his people, his heart was exceeding sorrowful. And…he went out and bowed himself down upon the earth, and cried mightily to his God, in behalf of his people; yea, those which were about to be destroyed because of their faith in the traditions of their fathers.*

—3 Nephi 9–11 (9–11)

The Lord responded when he told Nephi:

Lift up your head and be of good cheer: for behold, the time is at hand, and on this night shall the sign be given, and on the morrow come I into the world, to shew unto the world that I will fulfil all that I have caused to be spoken by the mouth of my Holy Prophets…for behold, at the going down of the sun, there was no darkness; and the people began to be astonished, because there was no darkness when the night came.

—3 Nephi 1:12–13, 17 (1:13, 15).

For such a significant event, the story must have been passed along for many years. According to a Mayan legend:

"Acxopil, at a very advanced age, determined to divide his empire into three kingdoms…and this division was made on a day when three suns were seen, which has caused some to think that it took place on the day of the birth of our Redeemer, a day on which it is commonly believed that such a meteor was observed."[95]

These "*three suns*" might have been based on 1) the sun setting, 2) a very bright meteor, and 3) the sunrise the following morning. The concept of a day of three suns could not have been taught to these indigenous people by early Christian missionaries. Add to that the fact that the time of the "*three suns*" was correlated to the time of Christ's birth.

THE WISE MEN

The Sons of Helaman

During the time before Jesus' birth, Helaman was a "*High Priest over the church*" (Alma 21:34 [46:6]). Helaman "*had two sons. He gave*

---

95   Bancroft. p. 566.

unto the eldest the name of Nephi, and unto the youngest the name of Lehi" (Helaman 2:19 [3:21]).

> *Behold, I* [Helaman] *have given unto you* [Nephi and Lehi] *the names of our first parents, which came out of the land of Jerusalem; and this I have done, that when you remember your names, that ye may remember them; and when ye remember them, ye may remember their works; and when ye remember their works, ye may know how that it is said, and also written, that they were good...*
>
> —Helaman 2:68 (5:6)

After Helaman's death, "*his eldest son Nephi began to reign in his stead*" (Helaman 2:33 [3:37]).

At one point, seeing the wickedness among the Nephites, Nephi grieved:

> *...O that I could have had my days, in the days when my father Nephi first came out of the land of Jerusalem, that I could have joyed with him in the promised land.*
>
> —Helaman 3:6 (7:7).

On another occasion, Nephi lamented, "*Our father Lehi was driven out of Jerusalem...*" (Helaman 3:58 [8:22]). Notice that Nephi refers to his ancestors, Lehi and Nephi, as his fathers. The Lord also promised this same Nephi:

> *Behold, I will bless thee forever; and I will make thee mighty in word and in deed, in faith and in works; yea, even that all things shall be done unto thee according to*

thy word, for thou shalt not ask that which is contrary to my will.

—Helaman 3:117 (10:5)

A Prophecy Given

Many years before the birth of Christ, according to the Book of Mormon, a prophecy was given:

> *...the Son of God cometh upon the face of the earth. And behold, he shall be born of Mary, at Jerusalem, which is the land of our forefathers, she being a Virgin, a precious and chosen vessel, who shall be overshadowed, and conceive by the power of the Holy Ghost, and bring forth a son, yea, even the Son of God...*

—Alma 5:18–19 (7:9–10)

Later, Samuel the Lamanite prophesied that another sign was to be given to indicate the time of Christ's birth, "*And behold there shall be a new star arise, such an one as ye never have beheld...*" (Helaman 5:59 [14:5]).

According to the Bible, Bethlehem would be the birthplace of Jesus (Micah 5:2). However, Micah lived over a century after Lehi's departure from the land of Jerusalem. Bethlehem is not mentioned anywhere in the Book of Mormon.

According to the Book of Mormon, the location of Jesus' birth reads "*at Jerusalem.*" It does not say "in Jerusalem." "*At Jerusalem*" would include the city and surrounding suburbs. Bethlehem is only a few miles south of Jerusalem.

Their Departure

The year came in which Samuel the Lamanite had prophesied that Christ would be born.

> *...Nephi...departed out of the land of Zarahemla, giving charge unto his son Nephi* [junior] *concerning the plates of brass, and all the records which had been kept...and all those things which had been kept sacred, from the departure of Lehi out of Jerusalem: then he departed out of the land, and whither he went, no man knoweth...*
>
> —3 Nephi 1:2–3 (1:2–3)

Also, nothing more was ever said about Nephi's brother, Lehi. Both Nephi and Lehi likely departed together since they had been traveling companions on their missionary journeys. Several years earlier, after delivering several prophecies, Samuel the Lamanite "*was never heard of more among the Nephites...*" (Helaman 5:120 [16:8]). All three disappeared from the Book of Mormon record at about the same time.

Nephi, Lehi, and Samuel knew Christ would be born at Jerusalem, and they knew of the sign of a new star. Aware of the prophecy regarding the time of Christ's birth, they may have had a yearning to be personal witnesses of this child of God.

The *Popol Vuh* states:

> *Balam-Quitzé, Balam-Acab, Mahucutah, and Iqui-Balam were pleased with their work; but the time had come when they had to withdraw from this world, and they announced their departure to their children. They gave them their last advice, gave them the symbol of royal power, and disappeared from sight... A short time later,*

the heirs of the three royal families undertook a journey to
the East, whence their parents had originally come.[96]

The *Popol Vuh* is naming four people who gave their children their "last advice," symbols of "royal power," and departed. Nephi gave charge or advice to his eldest son, symbols of royal power in the form of their ancient records, and departed. It is hard to deny the similarities between these two statements.

Although three people from the Book of Mormon were previously suggested, there is nothing that would prevent additional travelers from accompanying them.

Arrival in Jerusalem

After Christ's birth, according to the Book of Luke, Joseph took Mary and Jesus to the Temple in Jerusalem. The occasion would have been after Mary's required forty-day purification period. The arrival of the wise men had to be after that time since Joseph took Mary and Jesus to Egypt immediately after the wise men departed.

The Biblical account of the wise men (three is assumed only because there were three gifts) is found only in the Book of Matthew. Subsequent traditions gave them names and a theoretical origin.

While these wise men were aware of the birth of the king of the Jews at Jerusalem and the sign of a new star, they lacked any further details. When these travelers arrived in Jerusalem, they innocently went to King Herod.

In the time of King Herod…wise men from the East came
to Jerusalem, asking, "Where is the child who has been born

---

96   Goetz and Morley. (tr.). pp. 71–72.

king of the Jews? For we observed his star at its rising, and have come to pay him homage." When King Herod heard this, he was frightened, and all Jerusalem with him; and calling together all the chief priests and scribes of the people, he inquired of them where the Messiah was to be born. They told him, "In Bethlehem of Judea; for so it has been written by the prophet…

Matthew 2:1–5, NRSV

Wise men from the East may simply mean that they were foreigners. If these wise men were from the Americas, they probably spoke with a noticeable accent, perhaps a more ancient form of Hebrew. There is nothing to suggest that they needed someone to translate for them. Therefore, it seems they could still be understood.

It makes more sense for God to send members of his holy priesthood rather than pagan astrologers from Persia to welcome His son into this world and to provide confirmation to Joseph and Mary that their child was the Son of God.

According to the *Popol Vuh*, these people did eventually return. The Book of Mormon does not record their return. Nevertheless, the coincidences are fascinating.

SIGNS OF CHRIST'S DEATH

The Lamanite prophet, Samuel, not only prophesied of the signs that would be given to signify Christ's birth but he also prophesied of *"another sign I give unto you; yea, a sign of his death; for behold, he surely must die, that salvation may come…"* (Helaman 5:68 [14:14–15]).

Tropical Storm

Samuel, the Lamanite, prophesied:

> ...*the time that he* [Christ] *shall yield up the ghost, there shall be thunderings and lightnings for the space of many hours... And behold, there shall be great tempests...*
>
> —Helaman 5:77, 79 (14:21, 23)

The Nephites began counting the passage of years starting when the sign was given of Christ's birth. The Book of Mormon provides the time when Samuel's prophecy regarding Christ's death began to be fulfilled.

> *And it came to pass in the thirty and fourth year, in the first month, in the fourth day of the month, there arose a great storm, such an one as never had been known in all the land; and there was also a great and terrible tempest; and there was terrible thunder, insomuch that it did shake the whole earth as if it was about to divide asunder; and there was exceeding sharp lightnings, such as never had been known in all the land...*
>
> —3 Nephi 4:6–7 (8:5–7)

A typical thunderstorm lasts about thirty minutes. However, we are told that this storm lasted three hours (3 Nephi 4:16–17 [8:19]). This "great storm" was most likely an unusually large thunderstorm associated with a slow-moving cold front. It was probably not a hurricane since hurricanes typically occur later in the year and are rarely associated with lightning. The updrafts from a volcanic eruption can produce lightning and thunder.

*There were some which were carried away in the whirl-
wind; and whither they went, no man knoweth, save they
know that they were carried away.*

—3 Nephi 4:13 (8:16)

Tornadoes (whirlwinds) are often spawned within a
major thunderstorm.

The People Learn of the Aftermath

After the initial three hours of the storm and the beginnings of
earthquakes, the voice of the Lord spoke to them.

*And it came to pass that there was a voice heard among
all the inhabitants of the earth upon all the face of this
land, crying, Wo, wo, wo unto this people; wo unto the
inhabitants of the whole earth, except they shall repent,
for the Devil laugheth, and his angels rejoice, because of
the slain of the fair sons and daughters of my people; and
it is because of their iniquity and abominations that they
are fallen.*

—3 Nephi 4:26–27 (9:1–2)

The Lord went on to tell them of many cities that had been
destroyed along with descriptions of their abominations that justified
their destruction.

For this much destruction to have occurred so quickly, there
must have been a combination of a slow-moving thunderstorm along
with a volcanic eruption(s) and a major earthquake.

Volcanoes

Lightning or lava from an eruption can easily explain cities catching on fire, such as the cities of Zarahemla, Jacobugath, Laman, Josh, Gad, and Kishkumen (3 Nephi 4:8, 36, 38 [8:8, 9:9–10]). The Lord destroyed these cities "*because of their wickedness*" (3 Nephi 4:38 [9:10]). The widespread nature of so many cities catching on fire is more suggestive of volcanic activity. However, the term volcano does not occur in the Book of Mormon. As a more recently coined term, it would have been out of place.

In the mountainous area of Mexico, along the Pacific coast, there are numerous volcanoes. However, there are three volcanoes of interest associated with the lowland areas. El Chichón is closer to the southern Mayan area. Among the many eruptions of El Chichón, one is documented to have occurred about 2,000 years ago.[97] Another possibility is Mount Xitle. A nearby city, "*Cuicuilco was covered by lava 10 metres thick following the eruption of Mount Xitle in the 1st century AD.*"[98]

A third possible volcano is Popocatepetl. It is believed to have had a Plinian eruption about that time.

> *…between AD 50 and 100 the communities that dotted this slope of* [the volcano, Popocatepetl] *…were abruptly buried by a pumice-fall deposit that preserved the buildings, activity areas and agricultural fields but devastated*

---

97   J.M. Espindola, J.L. Macias, R.I. Tilling, and M.F. Sherida. "*Volcanic history of El Chichón Volcano (Chiapas, Mexico) during the Holocene, and its impact on human activity* (abstract)." Bulletin of Volcanology Vol. 62, No. 90. Jun 2000. <https://doi.org/10.1007/s004459900064> 30 May 2018.

98   Robin Heyworth. "History of Teotihuacan." *Uncovered History.* 13 Nov 2014. <https://uncoveredhistory.com/mexico/teotihuacan/history-of-teotihuacan/> 16 Oct 2019.

the settlements and made the region uninhabitable for generations to come.[99]

The largest and most violent of all the types of volcanic eruptions are Plinian eruptions… They release enormous amounts of energy and create eruption columns of gas and ash that can rise up to 50 km (35 miles) high at speeds of hundreds of meters per second. Ash from an eruption column can drift or be blown hundreds or thousands of miles away from the volcano.[100]

Since the dates given for these eruptions are approximate, they all fit well into the given time frame. Those who survived in decimated areas would have to migrate to a safer place where resources were available.

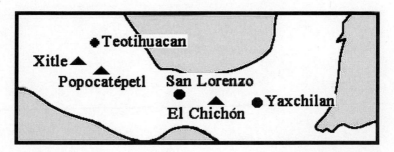

Construction [in Teotihuacán] *began with a huge ceremonial core and the building of three enormous pyramids in the 1st century AD. There was no progression, not even in the surrounding areas, and so it appears that the*

---

99   Patricia Plunket and Gabriela Uruñuela. "The archaeology of a Plinian eruption of the Popocatépetl volcano." *Geological Society, London, Special Publications.* 1 Jan 2000. <https://sp.lyellcollection.org/content/171/1/195> 17 Nov 2019.

100   Jessica Ball. "Types of Volcanic Eruptions" Geology.com <https://geology.com/volcanoes/types-of-volcanic-eruptions/> 9 Oct 2019.

Teotihuacáno [new migrants] *arrived with the knowledge to build on a scale never seen before in the Americas. Their first construction, the Pyramid of the Sun….*[101]

It would appear that shortly after the time of this eruption(s?), new people arrived in Teotihuacán to begin the construction of these grand pyramids. Although the construction of these pyramids may have begun in the first century A.D., it would take another two centuries before they were completed.[102]

Earthquakes

Samuel, the Lamanite, had prophesied of earthquakes.

…the earth shall quake and tremble, and the rocks which is upon the face of this earth, which is both above the earth and beneath, which ye know at this time is solid, or the more part of it is one solid mass, shall be broken up; yea, they shall be rent in twain, and shall ever after be found in seams, and in cracks, and in broken fragments upon the face of the whole earth; yea, both above the earth and both beneath….and there shall be many mountains laid low, like unto a valley, and there shall be many places, which are now called valleys, which shall become mountains, whose height thereof is great. And many highways shall be broken up, and many cities shall become desolate…

—Helaman 5:77–80 (14:21–24)

---

101   Heyworth. "History of Teotihuacan."

102   Owen Jarus. "Teotihuacan: Ancient City of Pyramids." *Live Science.* 20 Aug 2012. <https://www.livescience.com/22545-teotihuacan.html> 16 Oct 2019.

This prophecy was then fulfilled at the time of Christ's death when:

…highways were broken up, and the level roads were spoiled, and many smooth places became rough, and many great and noble cities were sunk, and many were burned, and many were shook till the buildings thereof had fallen to the earth, and the inhabitants thereof were slain, and the places were left desolate.

—3 Nephi 4:11 (8:13–14)

As described in the Book of Mormon, the inhabitants of the cities named Moronihah, Gilgal, Gadiandi, Gadiomnah, Jacob, and Gimgimno, were "*buried in the depths of the earth*" (3 Nephi 4:25–35 [8:25–9:8]). One possibility is that these people and their associated cities may have been buried by an avalanche. There is also another possibility. Stream valleys or swampy areas can act like quicksand during an earthquake—allowing buildings and people to literally sink into the ground. Interestingly, specific mention is made of the cities of Gilgal, Onihah, and Mocum sinking into the ground "*and the inhabitants thereof, and waters have I caused to come up in the stead thereof*" (3 Nephi 4:31–32 [9:6–7]).

[Mexico] sits atop three of the Earth's largest tectonic plates—the North American plate, the Cocos Plate, and the Pacific Plate. Whenever these chunks of crust grind or butt up against one another, earthquakes happen.… Mexico is one of the most seismically active countries in the world.[103]

---

103 Eric Brodwin. "Mexico is in the worst possible place for earthquakes—here's why it keeps getting hit." *Business Insider.* 16 Feb 2018. <https://www.businessinsider.com/why-mexico-earthquakes-science-2018-2> 5 Oct 2019.

Three Days of Darkness

Samuel had prophesied that:

...in that day that he [Christ] *shall suffer death, the sun shall be darkened and refuse to give his light unto you; and also the moon, and the stars; and there shall be no light upon the face of this land, even from the time that he shall suffer death, for the space of three days, to the time that he shall rise again from the dead;*

—Helaman 5:75–76 (14:20)

This prophecy was then fulfilled at the time of Christ's death when:

...there was thick darkness upon the face of all the land, insomuch that the inhabitants thereof which had not fallen, could feel the vapour of darkness; and there could be no light, because of the darkness, neither candles, neither torches; neither could there be fire kindled with their fine and exceeding dry wood, so that there could not be any light at all; and there was not any light seen, neither fire, nor glimmer, neither the sun, nor the moon, nor the stars, for so great were the mists of darkness which were upon the face of the land.

—3 Nephi 4:18–20 (8:20–22)

[Volcanic] *ashfall can cause partial or complete darkness by blocking sunlight. Depending on several factors, including the size and duration of an eruption, strength and direction of the wind, and distance from the volcano, an area may experience dark conditions for as little as a few minutes or as long as 1–3 days.*[104]

Volcanic action is an easy explanation for this prophesied "*mists of darkness.*" However, some earthquakes can also produce large quantities of dark heavy gases. Sunlight can be completely blocked out. These gases do not support combustion. "*Large eruptions can block the sun, cause acid rain and thunder/lighting, and even suffocate nearby residents.*"[105]

For such significant events, legends must have been passed along for many years.

> *One hundred and sixteen years after this regulation or inventions of the Toltec calendar,* "*the sun and moon were eclipsed, the earth shook, and the rocks were rent asunder, and many other things and signs happened, though there was no loss of life. This was in the year…which, the chronology being reduced to our systems, proves to be the same date when Christ our Lord suffered.*"[106]

The concept of an eclipse of the sun and moon associated with an earthquake could not have been taught to these indigenous people by Christian missionaries. Add to that the fact that the event was correlated to the time of Christ's crucifixion.

---

104 "Volcano Hazards Program." *U.S. Geological Survey.* 20 Dec 1999. <https://volcanoes.usgs.gov/Imgs/Jpg/SoufHills/32424296-060_caption.html> 30 May 2018.

105 Ethan Siegel. "'Volcanic Ash' Isn't Actually Ash." *Forbes.* 23 Aug 2018. <https://www.forbes.com/sites/startswithabang/2018/04/23/volcanic-ash-isnt-actually-ash/#244222de3dc1> 7 Oct 2018.

106 Bancroft. p. 210.

The suggestion that there was no loss of life implies that those who recorded that portion of their history were far enough away from the center of the greater damage. From the statements given in the Book of Mormon, it would seem that the people at this location were among the more righteous.

> The weird phenomena which accompany major earthquakes were absolutely unknown in 1830. There was no science of seismology [study of earthquakes] at that time, yet the Book of Mormon records in their proper sequence the phenomena that accompany the great upheavals.[107]

It is unlikely that Joseph Smith Jr. ever experienced any major earthquake. For the Book of Mormon to provide so many accurate descriptions means that it had to have come from eyewitness accounts.

CHRIST VISITED AMERICA

The Book of Mormon recounts Christ visiting the people when they

> ...cast their eyes up again towards Heaven, and...they saw a man descending out of Heaven: and he was clothed in a white robe, and he came down and stood in the midst of them....he stretched forth his hand, and spake unto the people, saying: Behold I am Jesus Christ, of which the prophets testified that should come into the world;
>
> —3 Nephi 5:9–11 (11:8–10)

---

107   Roy Weldon. *Other Sheep*. Independence, MO: Herald Publishing House, 1958. p. 66.

Christ then allowed those assembled to see and touch the wounds in His hands, His feet, and His side. Christ then taught them repentance and authorized certain individuals to baptize in His name. He went on to heal the sick, bless the children, and teach the same doctrine he had previously taught in the areas in and around Galilee and Jerusalem.

It appears that legends followed his departure. Similarities to Christ's teachings became associated with a historic spiritual leader variously known as Quetzalcoatl, Kukulcan, or Gucumatz. All these names translate to mean feathered serpent. The name, Quetzalcoatl, also came to be used as a title for spiritual leaders. [Quetzalcoatl] *"was regarded as the god of winds and rain and as the creator of the world and mankind."*[108] From another source: *"As the morning and evening star, Quetzalcoatl was the symbol of death and resurrection."*[109]

> *The Mesoamericans were quick to take to the new faith of Christianity. They appear to have seen in the worship of Jesus Christ a similarity to the cult of the Plumed Serpent, Quetzalcoatl. Jesus's teachings on brotherly love were in harmony with Topiltzin-Quetzalcoatl's pious and peaceful government, while the Christian idea of the second coming clearly resonated with the ancient Mesoamerican myth of Quetzalcoatl's departure and promised return. In an unlikely marriage of faiths, the Plumed Serpent became closely associated with Christ.*[110]

108   Mark Cartwright. "Quetzalcoatl." *Ancient History Encyclopedia.* 1 Aug 2013. <https://www.ancient.eu/Quetzalcoatl/> 30 Nov 2019.

109   Adela. "Quetzalcóatl Meso-American God." *Naked History.* 21 Dec 2015. <http://www.historynaked.com/quetzalcoatl-meso-american-god/> 30 Nov 2019.

110   Charles Phillips. *The Complete Illustrated History: Aztec & Maya.* NY: Metro Books. 2008. p. 76.

Quetzalcoatl as a culture hero is also found in the ancient Maya texts as Kukulcán and as Gucumatz among the Quichés. All these myths insist that even though Quetzalcoatl went away, he was to return. The god and the priest, often confused in native thinking, continued through the ages as a symbol of the most lofty spiritual thought in ancient Mexico.[111]

CONCLUSION

Events described in the Bible and Book of Mormon combined with geography and the histories and legends of the Mayans provide us with compatible stories. Taken together, all these things complement and support the events described in the Book of Mormon. I believe these were...

REAL PEOPLE IN REAL PLACES!

---

111   Miguel León-Portilla. *Pre-Columbian Literatures of Mexico.* Norman, University of Oklahoma Press, 1969. p. 33.

CHAPTER 9:

DISCOVERING MORMON IN MAYAN HISTORY

Introduction

Deciphering native legends regarding events that occurred more than sixteen hundred years ago is very challenging. Names were frequently reused among the Mayans to the extent that a popular leader's name may have subsequently been used as a title. Centuries later, the stories of different individuals using the same name may have been combined into one legendary account.

Bancroft often suggests specific years for certain events that occurred centuries before Columbus' arrival in America. At one point, Bancroft refers to Hueman, the secondary subject of this chapter, as living "*toward the end of the seventh century.*"[112] In another place, Bancroft states that Hueman "*departed from Huehue Tlapallan...in the fifth or sixth century.*"[113] However, in a footnote, he states that "*Ixtlilxochitl... says* [this same event] *was 305 years after the death of Christ or about 338 A.D.*"[114] In another place, Bancroft stated that Hueman "*was now three hundred years old.*"[115] In various places, he acknowledged a lack of

---

112   Hubert H. Bancroft. *The Works of Hubert Howe Bancroft,* Vol. V, *The Native Races, Primitive History.* San Francisco, CA: A. L. Bancroft & Co., Publishers, 1883. p. 242.

113   Ibid. p. 211.

114   Ibid. p. 211.

115   Ibid. p. 251.

reliability, as different dates were proposed for the same event. These problems are the result of stories being passed along through many generations over many centuries. Caution is necessary since legends can often grow and change with time. For this work, specific years based on legendary history will be considered questionable unless supported by multiple sources or archaeological evidence.

Book of Mormon Years[116]

Where Mormon wrote of those things that occurred during his life, his suggested time frames would be more reliable. However, the years, as described in the Book of Mormon cannot be the solar years with which we are familiar. To understand the dilemma and find a solution, a comparison of ancient calendars is needed.

The Bible (2 Kings 24) describes the coronation of Zedekiah. *"Mattaniah, whose name was changed to Zedekiah, was put on the throne by Nebuchadnezzar in 597* [B.C.]."[117]

> *"...after Zedekiah became king: (1) Lehi had a vision; (2) Lehi began to prophesy; (3) Lehi is persecuted;* [and] *(4) Lehi escaped into the wilderness..."*[118]

Lehi sent his sons back to Jerusalem to retrieve the brass plates—a history of the people combined with their scriptures. After they returned with the plates, Lehi saw that the plates contained, among other things,

---

116   Terry O'Leary. "Book of Mormon Years." *The Witness*, No. 134. Independence, MO, Book of Mormon Foundation, *Summer 2010.* p. 3–9.

117   Emil G. Hirsch, et al. "Nebuchadnezzar." *Jewish Encyclopedia.* 1906. <http://www.jewishencyclopedia.com/articles/11407-nebuchadnezzar> 11 Oct 2019.

118   O'Leary. p. 6.

"*a record of Jews from the beginning, even down to the commencement of the reign of Zedekiah...*" (1 Nephi 1:161 [5:12]).

Several months must have passed after Zedekiah became king for all of these things to have occurred. That would place Lehi's departure around the spring of 596 B.C.

Christ was born in Bethlehem during the time of Herod the Great. We are repeatedly told that "*King Herod the Great...died in* [March/April] *4 B.C.*"[119] Therefore, if Christ was born in 5 B.C., That would be slightly more than 591 years after Lehi left Jerusalem. However, according to the Book of Mormon, 600 years would pass between the time that Lehi left Jerusalem and the time that Christ was born.[120] How did 591+ years become 600 years? The answer lies in the fact that different calendars were used.

The Biblical calendar consists of twelve months of thirty days/month. This is seen in the story of Noah. That great flood began on the seventeenth day of the second month and ended on the seventeenth day of the seventh month. We are told that this all took place in 150 days (Gen. 7:11; 8:3–4). In other words, "*five months equaled 150 days or thirty days per month.*"[121] At the other end of the Bible in the Book of Revelation, a period of time was given as 3½ years (written as "*a time, and times, and half a time*" [Rev. 12:14]) or 42 months (Rev. 13:5) or 1,260 days (Rev. 11:3; 12:6). This would be equivalent to twelve months per year and thirty days per month. This is sometimes referred to as the Biblical calendar.

---

119   "King Herod the Great plans how to kill Jesus." *Bibleview.* <https://bibleview.org/en/bible/birthofjesus/angryherod/> 11 Oct 2019.

120   1 Nephi 3:4; 5:236 (10:4; 19:8); 2 Nephi 11:35 (25:19)

121   O'Leary, p. 4

It is interesting that Moses, who wrote the book of Genesis, grew up in Egypt. An early Egyptian calendar consisted of twelve months and each month consisted of three ten-day weeks or thirty days. Egypt adopted the 365-day calendar during the eighth century B.C. This was done by adding five days at the end of each year to better correlate with the solar year.[122] However, the 360-day calendar probably continued to be used as a religious calendar.

The Mayans used three different calendars: (1) 260-day Tzolk'in calendar, (2) a 365-day Haab calendar and (3) a Long Count Calendar. The first two, combined, created a 52-year cycle that was not generally used to record longer periods. The third calendar was used to record the passage of days spanning thousands of years. It consisted, in part of twenty-day months (called a uinal). Eighteen months (called a tun) was a 360-day vague or approximate year.

Notice that there is a common thread among all three of these calendars. All used a 360-day vague or approximate year. It was noted above that the time between Lehi's departure and the birth of Christ was 600 years—according to the Book of Mormon. If those 600 years were 360-day vague or approximate years and we convert that to 365.25-day solar years, it is equal to 591.4 years. This is a perfect solution to show Lehi leaving Jerusalem in the spring of 596 B.C. and Christ being born 600 vague years later in the fall of 5 B.C.—supporting the validity of the Book of Mormon.

$$\frac{360 \text{ days / vague year} \times 600 \text{ vague years}}{365.25 \text{ days / solar year}} = 591.4 \text{ solar years}$$

122   Frank Praise, ed. *The Book of Calendars*. New York, Facts on File, Inc., 1982. p. 126.

As I continue, there will be incidents in the archaeological record in which a date is provided using the standard solar year calendar. As a matter of correlating those dates with the Book of Mormon, I will be converting those dates to Book of Mormon vague years. This will be done by using the fall of 5 B.C. as the beginning point and then calculating forward based on 360-day vague years. It should be noted, when calculating between dates given as B.C. and those given as A.D., there is no year zero. For example, a child born in 2 B.C. would celebrate his third birthday in A.D. 2.

Hill Cumorah

The location of the Hill Cumorah, as mentioned in the Book of Mormon, will play a role in this sequence of events. The exact location of that hill has been endlessly debated by many Mormon scholars. For varying reasons, I believe that the mountain known as Cerro Rabon in Oaxaca, Mexico fits the geography illustrated here.

Richard DeLong published an article indicating certain Mayan glyphs and the local Mayan dialect pointing to Cerro Rabon as the Book of Mormon "hill Ramah" or "Hill Cumorah."[123] The "hill Ramah" (Ether 6:83 [(15:11)]) was the Jaredite reference to the same hill that the Nephites called "Hill Camorah"[124] (Mormon 3:3–8 [6:2–6]).

The Hill Cumorah is where Mormon hid many of the sacred records of his ancestors. The final major battle between the Nephites and Lamanites took place in the land of Cumorah—at the base of that hill.

---

123   Richard A. DeLong. "Maya Glyphs May Identify Hill Cumorah." *The Witness, No.* 67. Independence, MO: Book of Mormon Foundation, Winter 1989. pp. 4–5.

124   The Book of Mormon quotes are from the 1830 edition in which the name of the hill is spelled "Camorah." Subsequent editions have changed the spelling to "Cumorah."

According to Neil Steede:

In the foothills of Jalapa de Diaz [near Cerro Rabon]…
*there are no ruins and there really are no pyramids, yet we
do know it* [was] *a wide battlefield as almost anyone who
lives in the outlying areas of Jalapa has found hatchets or
obsidian knives, but always weapons.*[125]

INTRODUCING MORMON AND HUEMAN

Mormon

The focus of this chapter is on the life of Mormon. His involvement with the historic records began with Ammaron.

*And it came to pass that when three hundred and twenty
years had passed away, Ammaron, being constrained by
the Holy Ghost, did hide up the records which were sacred;
yea, even all the sacred records which had been handed
down from generation to generation, which were sacred,
even until the three hundred and twentieth year from the
coming of Christ.*

—4 Nephi 1:57–58 (1:48).

During that same year, he went to Mormon, who was in his tenth year, and told him,

*…I perceive that thou art a sober child, and art quick
to observe; therefore, when ye are about twenty and four*

---

125   Edwardo Corvantes Brava. "United States Citizens Assure that the Hill Rabon Contains Sacred Maya Writings." *Tuxtepec, Mexico newspaper* [English translation]. 12 Apr 2005. <http://www.freerepublic.com/focus/religion/2522214/replies?c=951> 20 Oct 2019.

years old, I would that ye should remember the things that
ye have observed concerning this people; and when ye are
of that age, go to the land of Antum, unto a hill, which is
called Shim; and there have I deposited unto the Lord, all
the sacred engravings concerning this people. And behold,
ye shall take the [large] plates of Nephi unto yourself, and
the remainder shall ye leave in the place where they are;
and ye shall engrave upon the plates of Nephi, all the
things which ye have observed concerning this people.

—Mormon 1:2–5 (1:2–4)

When he told Mormon to go to the hill Shim in the land of Antum, it must have been a very different place from where he was living at the time. For this young boy to remember many years later where the sacred plates were deposited would mean that it must have been a well-known area and the hiding place would be easy to recall.

During the following year, Mormon's father took Mormon southward to the land of Zarahemla. Mormon was impressed when he saw countless buildings covering the land occupied by a very large population (Mormon 1:7 [1:6–7]).

When he was a teenager, Mormon had a strong spiritual experience that led him to a lifelong dedication to the Lord. Years later, he wrote of that experience.

And I, being fifteen years of age, and being somewhat of a
sober mind, therefore, I was visited of the Lord, and tasted,
and knew of the goodness of Jesus. And I did endeavor to
preach unto this people, but my mouth was shut, and I
were forbidden that I should preach unto them: for behold
they had willfully rebelled against their God... And it

came to pass in that same year, there began to be a war
again between the Nephites and the Lamanites.

—Mormon 1:16–18, 21 (1:15–17, 2:1)

Hueman

The writings of Ixtlilxóchitl, *The Works of Hubert Howe Bancroft* and the *Popol Vuh* will continue to be examined. These sources make references to a man who was variously referred to as Hueman, Huematzin or Huemac. It appears his name was Hueman and Matzin was his title. Later in life, perhaps after his retirement, it appears that he was referred to as Huemac. He was described as both a spiritual leader and a military leader.

Huematzin, or King Hueman, is called the King of Tezcuco. Tezcuco is near Teotihuacán.

> *Fernando de Alva Ixtlilxóchitl was a grandson of the last king of Tezcuco, from whom he inherited all that were saved of the records in the public archives. His works are more extensive than those of any other native writer, covering the whole ground of Nahua history, although treating more particularly of the Chichimecs, his ancestors.*[126]

Ixtlilxóchitl, as a grandson of the last king of Tezcuco, probably had a vested interest in these historic records. He may have felt a kinship with this ancestral king of Tezcuco, Huematzin.

What follows are the intertwined histories of Mormon and Hueman. Although there is some conjecture, it is supported by

---

126   Bancroft. p. 147.

archaeological findings and historical records. The parallels between the life of Mormon and Hueman are fascinating.

MILITARY LEADERS

Mormon, Leader of the Army—A.D. 326–330[127]

> *Therefore, it came to pass that in my sixteenth year, I did go forth at the head of an army of the Nephites, against the Lamanites; therefore three hundred and twenty and six years had passed away.*

> —Mormon 1:23 (2:2)

The Nephites had started counting their years from the time that the sign was given of the birth of the Savior. As I continue, the correlation between that number of years and Mormon's age will allow for an estimation of his age during the coming events.

Mormon at the head of an army as a teenager? His large stature may have given him some credibility (Mormon 1:22 [2:1]). However, that alone would not be enough to justify placing him at the head of an army. He was too young to have proven himself on the battlefield, especially since this war began just a year earlier. If we see Mormon's father as a strong military and spiritual leader, it would be easier to understand how his son came to…

- the attention of Ammaron regarding the protection of a national treasure (Mormon 1:5 [1:4]),

- have a strong spiritual experience at a young age (Mormon 1:16 [1:15]),

---

127 Based on the Book of Mormon 360-day vague years

- be taught how to read and write in their ancient system of writing (Mormon 1:2 [1:2]), and

- be at the head of an army at such a young age (Mormon 1:23 [2:2]).

Four years later, the Lamanite King's army of 44,000 came against Mormon's army of 42,000. The Lamanite army was defeated and fled (Mormon 1:31–33 [2:9]). Mormon, now in his twentieth year, was proving himself in battle.

Hueman, a Great Leader—A.D. 338

According to Ixtlilxóchitl, Hueman became a great leader of the people of Bountiful Land—305 years after the eclipse of the sun and the moon.[128] It is assumed here that these 305 years were Mayan long count years or 360-day vague years. If that eclipse equated to the time of Christ's death, that would have been about A.D. 33 (in Book of Mormon years). Ixtlilxóchitl also relates that the people left Bountiful Land that same year.[129] Then 305 years later would have been about A.D. 338 (in Book of Mormon years). Hueman's departure from their homeland and becoming a great leader during the same year would suggest that the previous leader had retired, passed away, or was killed in battle.

---

128   G. Ashe, et al. *The Quest for America.* New York: Praeger Publishers, 1971. p. 232.

129   Bancroft. p. 211.

DRIVEN NORTHWARD BY THEIR ENEMIES

Mormon—A.D. 331–345[130]

Mormon's account never mentioned any specific event in A.D. 338–339. However, during the years of A.D. 331–345, he described a time when he saw the sadness in his people and thought that they had begun to repent of their iniquities (Mormon 1:34 [2:10]).

> *But behold this my joy was in vain, for their sorrowing was not unto repentance, because of the goodness of God, but it was rather the sorrowing of the damned, because the Lord would not always suffer them to take happiness in sin. And they did curse God and wish to die. Nevertheless, they would struggle with the sword for their lives…and I saw that the day of grace was past with them, both temporally and spiritually: for I saw thousands of them hewn down in open rebellion against their God, and heaped up as dung upon the face of the land.… And…in the three hundred and forty and fifth year, the Nephites did begin to flee before the Lamanites, and they were pursued until they came even to the land of Jashon, before it were possible to stop them in their retreat.*

> —Mormon 1:37–42 (2:13–16)

The Nephites were being driven northward past the narrow neck of land (Isthmus of Tehuantepec).

---

130   Based on the Book of Mormon 360-day vague years.

And now the city of Jashon was near the land where Ammaron had deposited the records unto the Lord, that they might not be destroyed

—Mormon 1:43 (2:17a).

RETRIEVING THE LARGE PLATES OF NEPHI

Mormon—A.D. 345[131]

Ammaron had advised Mormon to retrieve the large plates of Nephi when he was about twenty-four years old. However, his involvement as a military leader during the animosities between the Nephites and Lamanites would have made it difficult. Mormon recorded that in his thirty-fifth year, he

> *...had gone according to the word of Ammaron, and taken the* [large] *plates of Nephi, and did make a record according to the words of Ammaron.*
>
> —Mormon 1:44 (2:17)

As directed by Ammaron, Mormon retrieved only the large plates of Nephi. The remaining records were left in place. Mormon was to add to the large plates *"all the things* [he] *observed concerning this people"* (Mormon 1:5 [1:4]).

During that same year, some of the Nephites were being hunted and driven *"northward to the land which was called Shem"* (Mormon 1:48 [2:20]). Any Nephites who had settled near the narrow neck were being pushed further northward. The Nephites gathered their people

---

131   Based on the Book of Mormon 360-day vague years

together and fortified the city of Shem, hoping to take a stand against the Lamanites

THE BATTLES CONTINUE

Mormon—A.D. 346-349[132]

During the 346th year (Mormon would have been in his thirty-sixth year), the Lamanites began to attack. Mormon had given strong encouragement to his army by urging them to *"fight for their wives, and their children, and their houses and their homes"* (Mormon 1:51[2:23]). That had a positive effect on the men because his army of 30,000 was able to defeat the Lamanite army of 50,000.

While the Lamanites had suffered a serious defeat, Mormon still saw some weaknesses among his troops (Mormon 1:56–57 [2:26]).

> *But behold we did go forth against the Lamanites...until we had again taken possession of the lands of our inheritance. And the three hundred and forty and ninth year had passed away.*
>
> —Mormon 1:58–59 (2:27–28).

Hueman

Hueman and the associated exiles from Huehue Tlapallan were being driven further northward past the narrow neck of land. Bancroft described this withdrawal. Hueman and all of:

> *...the exiles from Huehue Tlapallan* [ancient Bountiful Land] *were tarrying at Tulancingo, where they had*

---

132   Based on the Book of Mormon 360-day vague years

arrived…and where—contrary to the advice of their prophet Hueman, if we may credit the tradition—weary with their long wanderings, they lived…in a house which they built sufficiently large to accommodate them all…[133]

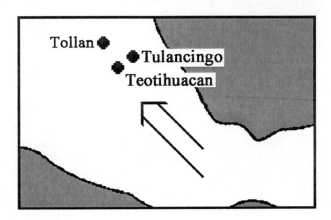

In a determination to remain close to their homeland, some of the Toltecs (Nephites) probably settled a short distance north of the narrow neck. However, no such luxury could be granted to the leaders whose lives were more seriously threatened. For their safety, they had to settle further northward close to a large population of allies.

After negotiating with the leaders in nearby places and under Hueman's leadership, they:

> *…transferred their home to…Tula…where they founded the city of Tollan, where now stands the little village of Tula, about thirty miles north-west of the city of Mexico.*[134]

If Hueman was the man we call Mormon, then this may have been closer to the area where he grew up. He would have been more

---

133   Bancroft. p. 213.

134   Ibid. p. 243.

familiar with the surroundings and felt safer. He also would have been aware of available resources.

Tollan was close to Teotihuacán where more people and resources would be available for war preparations. *"Several areas with extensive obsidian-working debris on the surface have been found in Teotihuacán."*[135] Teotihuacán generally controlled the obsidian trade in that area. Obsidian was primarily used for making tools but also would include the production of arrowheads and spear tips.

The city of Teotihuacán *"was founded at about the time of Christ in a small but fertile valley opening onto the northeast side of the Valley of Mexico."*[136] In Teotihuacán, the Pyramid of the Sun had been completed in A.D. 200 and the Pyramid of the Moon had been completed in A.D. 250.[137] *"The pyramid* [Temple of the Feathered Serpent] *is believed to have been completed sometime in the 3rd century AD."*[138]

> *This temple* [of the Feathered Serpent] *was an important point of pilgrimage for the city's ancient inhabitants who would worship and conduct rituals at its location.*[139]

As mentioned in the preceding chapter, there appears to be a correlation between the ideology espoused by Quetzalcoatl (or Feathered

---

135 Michael W. Spence. *The Obsidian Industry of Teotihuacan.* American Antiquity Vol 32, No. 4, 1967. p. 507.

136 Michael D. Coe. *The Maya,* 7th ed. New York: Thames & Hudson, 2005.

137 Fern Coll. "Exploring the Teotihuacan Pyramids in Mexico." *Chimu Blog.* <http://search.pollicare.com/?t=1807&ap=1478616638660322&r=213807bde8e333aef-66119f5815b63a2&hp=1> 16 Oct 2019.

138 Owen Jarus. "Teotihuacan: Ancient City of Pyramids." *Live Science.* 20 Aug 2012. <https://www.livescience.com/22545-teotihuacan.html> 16 Oct 2019.

139 "Teotihuacan, The New World's First Great City." *Mexonline.com.* <http://www.mex-online.com/history-teotihuacan.htm> 17 Oct 2019.

Serpent) and the teachings of Christ. This Temple of the Feathered Serpent may have been their version of a place of worship.

At the time that Hueman arrived in the area, Teotihuacán was well established.

TEN YEAR TRUCE

Nephite and Lamanite Truce—A.D. 350[140]

> *…in the three hundred and fiftieth year, we made a treaty with the Lamanites…in which we did get the lands of our inheritance divided. And the Lamanites did give unto us the land northward; yea, even to the narrow passage which led into the land southward. And we did give unto the Lamanites all the land southward.*
>
> —Mormon 1:59–62 (2:28–29)

The treaty that was agreed upon meant that "*…the Lamanites did not come to battle again until ten years more had passed away*" (Mormon 1:63 [3:1]).

During the truce, the Lamanites retreated southward past the narrow passage—the Isthmus of Tehuantepec. Some Nephites may have felt comfortable settling in or near the Land Desolation and closer to the Isthmus of Tehuantepec and their original homeland. Any Nephites who were still living in the land southward would have been required to move or perhaps become vassals in submission to the Lamanite rulers.

---

140   Based on the Book of Mormon 360-day vague years

Toltec (Nephite) Truce

Bancroft recorded a very similar scenario.

> *Unable to resist this formidable army, the Toltec* [Nephite] *king was compelled to send ambassadors bearing rich presents to sue for peace... The presents were received, but no satisfactory agreement seems to have been made at first... Ixtlilxóchitl speak*[s] *vaguely of a truce that was concluded as a result of this or a subsequent embassy, to the effect that the Toltecs* [Nephites] *should not be molested for ten years, an old military usage requiring that ten years should always intervene between the declaration of war and the commencement of hostilities; and the latter states that the army was withdrawn in the meantime, because sufficient supplies could not be obtained in the territory of the Toltecs.*[141]

The lack of supplies *"in the territory of the Toltecs"* may be referring to those who were further south. They would have been closer to the narrow neck and closer to the front lines of the impending battle. They were also further away from their supply of obsidian weapons.

Traditions Agree

The Toltec had a tradition of a ten–year truce to allow each side to prepare for their final battle. Joseph Smith could not have known of this law during the translation of the Book of Mormon. Nevertheless, during the truce, we are told that Mormon *"had employed* [his] *people, the Nephites, in preparing their lands and their arms against the time of battle"* (Mormon 1:64 [3:1]).

---

141   Bancroft. p. 279.

TRUCE COMES TO AN END

End of Nephite Truce—A.D. 360[142]

The burdens on Mormon's shoulders were growing. He had been leading his people while involved in an ongoing war. He had dealt with a history of successes and huge losses that had forced his people to move to new territories. The ten-year truce had been a time of preparation. Mormon would also have been adding to the history of his people on the large plates of Nephi. The time for the truce to end had finally arrived.

> *...after the tenth year had passed away, making in the whole, three hundred and sixty years from the coming of Christ, the king of the Lamanites sent an epistle unto me* [Mormon], *which gave unto me to know that they were preparing to come again to battle against us...I did cause my people that they should gather themselves together at the land Desolation, to a city which was in the borders, by the narrow pass which lead into the land southward. And there we did place our armies, that we might stop the armies of the Lamanites, that they might not get possession of any of our lands; therefore, we did fortify against them with all our force.*
>
> —Mormon 1:68–69 (3:4–6)

The fact that the king of the Lamanites sent such a letter to Mormon is confirmation that Mormon was considered by them to be the chief military leader of the Nephites.

---

142   Based on the Book of Mormon 360-day vague years

End of Toltec Truce

Hueman may have chosen another leader to help carry the burden. His choice may have been the person whom the Toltecs called Acxitl, a son of Hueman.[143] If Hueman and Mormon refer to the same person, then this son of Hueman may have been their name for Mormon's son, Moroni. Acxitl may have become the second in command and a courier in the negotiations.

Bancroft described the end of the ten-year truce as follows:

> *According to the Spanish writers, the ten years' truce concluded between Acxitl* [Hueman's son] *and his foes under the command of Huehuetzin* [Lamanite], *was now about to expire, and the rebel prince...appeared at the head of an immense army, ready to submit his differences with the Toltec* [Nephite] *king to the arbitration of the battle-field.*[144]

MILITARY RETIREMENT

Mormon Retired—A.D. 362[145]

For a time, the Nephites were successful. However, Mormon was upset with the wickedness among his people. After tasting some success, they swore

> *...before the heavens that they would avenge themselves of the blood of their brethren which had been slain.... And they did swear by the heavens, and also by the throne of*

---

143   Bancroft. p. 270.

144   Ibid. p. 282.

145   Based on the Book of Mormon 360-day vague years

God, that they would go up to battle against their enemies, and would cut them off from the face of the land. And it came to pass that I, Mormon, did utterly refuse from this time forth, to be a commander and a leader of this people, because of their wickedness and abomination.

—Mormon 1:74–76 (3:9–11)

While Mormon was not in command of the armies, he probably had more time to record his observations of his people. As such, he would continue monitoring the ongoing battles, both successes and losses. He saw the growing threats of the destruction of his people while also becoming concerned for the safety of the records of his people.

Hueman Retired

No reference has been found to indicate that Hueman retired from leading his army. However, he must have retired since, as will be seen later in this chapter, we are told that he came out of retirement.

RETRIEVAL OF THE RECORDS

Hill Shim

The Lamanites were getting closer to the hill Shim where Ammaron had hidden "*all the sacred records which had been handed down from generation to generation*" (4 Nephi 1:58 [1:48]). Mormon became concerned regarding the safety of those sacred records. At this point, it is helpful to understand the approximate location of hill Shim.

In the ongoing battles between the Nephites and Lamanites, Mormon wrote:

...the Lamanites did come down against the city of Desolation; and there was an exceeding sore battle fought in the land Desolation, in which they did beat the Nephites. And they fled again from before them, and they came to the city Beaz...the Nephites were driven and slaughtered with an exceeding great slaughter...the Nephites did again flee from before them, taking all the inhabitants with them, both in towns and villages.

—Mormon 2:21–24 (4:19–22)

The city of Desolation was near that narrow neck of land which had been the border between the Nephites and Lamanites during the ten-year truce. As the Nephites were pushed further northward past the city of Desolation, the Lamanites must have been getting closer to the hill Shim.

Other than the references by Mormon, there is one other reference to the Hill Shim in the Book of Ether. It helps to establish an approximate location of that hill. As Moroni abridged the Jaredite history, he wrote:

the Lord warned Omer in a dream, that he should depart out of the land; wherefore Omer departed out of the land with his family, and travelled many days, and came over and passed by the hill of Shim, and came over by the place where the Nephites were destroyed, and from thence eastward, and came to a place which was called Ablom, by the seashore, and there he pitched his tent....

—Ether 4:3–4 (9:3)

The Jaredite, Omer, had been told by the Lord to escape from a cruel King. The site from which he departed was probably San Lorenzo. Most of the area through which Omer and his family would have traveled would have been forested flatlands. After covering about one hundred miles, they would have encountered the foothills of the nearby mountains. Many of these hills consist of long ridges extending out from the mountains, ending in gentle slopes onto the plains below. Hill Shim was probably one of these prominent ridges or an isolated nearby hill. It is also interesting that these Jaredites "*passed by the hill Shim*" (Ether 4:3 [9:3]). This would suggest that they walked in the plains around the base of that hill. This description fits the proposed geography.

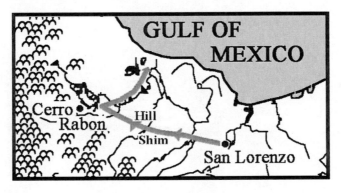

As they traveled, they went toward the "*place where the Nephites were destroyed*" (Ether 4:4 [9:3]). From Moroni's viewpoint, this must have been referring to the area around Hill Cumorah/Cerro Rabon.

Omer and his family then turned eastward (northeast) to a place by the seashore (Ether 4:4 [9:3]). From Cerro Rabon, they could have easily followed the Papaloapan River and then pitched their tents near the Alvarado Lagoon that empties into the Gulf of Mexico.

Mormon Retrieves All the Records

And now I, Mormon, seeing that the Lamanites were about to overthrow the land, therefore I did go to the hill Shim, and did take all the records which Ammaron had hid up unto the Lord.

—Mormon 2:25 (4:23)

The Lamanites were getting too close for comfort! Mormon, concerned for the safety of the remaining records, and contrary to Ammoron's advice, retrieved all the records of his people.

Huematzin Gathered the Chronicles of His People

According to the *Popol Vuh*:

Huematzin, the king of Tezcuco, had gathered together all the chronicles of the Tolteca in the Teoamoxtli, or "Divine Book," which contained the legends of the creation of the world, the emigration from Asia of those peoples, the stops on the Journey, the dynasty of their kings, their social and religious institutions, their sciences, arts, and so on....[146]

And this was the life of the Quiché, because no longer can be seen [the sacred book that they called the *Popol Vuh*] *which the kings had in olden times, for it has disappeared.*[147]

---

146 T. D. Goetz and S. G. Morley, translators, from the translation of Adrian Recinos. *Popol Vuh, The Sacred Book of the Ancient Quiche Maya.* Norman, Oklahoma; University of Oklahoma Press, 1950. p. 9.

147 Ibid. pp. 234–235.

Bancroft also described the involvement of Hueman and a book of God. It looks like two descriptions of the same person and the same sacred book.

> [At]...*a meeting of all the sages under the direction of the aged Hueman...there were brought forward all the Toltec records reaching back to the earliest period of their existence, and from these documents, after a long conference and the most careful study, the Teoamoxtli, or "book of God," was prepared. In its pages were inscribed the Nahua annals from the time of the deluge, or even from the creation; together with all their religious rites, governmental system, laws and social customs; their knowledge respecting agriculture and all the arts and sciences, particular attention being given to astrology* [religion]; *and a complete explanation of their modes of reckoning time and interpreting the hieroglyphics. To the divine book was added a chapter of prophecies respecting the future events and the signs by which it would be known when the time of their fulfillment was drawing near.*[148]

A third source also connects Hueman with a "divine book."

> *According to the tradition registered by the seventeenth-century indigenous chronicler Ixtlilxóchitl, it was Huemac (also written as Hueman o*[r] *Huematzin), ruler of the ancient realm of Tollan (Tula Hidalgo)...who brought together the cultural knowledge and memory of his time in*

---

148   Ibid. p. 251.

a book (or rather set of books), which was called teo-amax-tli, i.e. "divine book" or "book of the divine."[149]

This last source confirms the idea that the names Hueman, Huematzin, and Huemac originally referred to the same individual. The names, Hueman or Huemac, may have eventually become a "*Toltec title, likely to simply mean either 'The Elder', or simply Chief Priest*."[150]

These sources also support the suggestion that Hueman or Huemac was the author of that "divine book."

Another source also describes an early sacred book. It was written in 1723 by a Catholic friar, over a century before the Book of Mormon was published. Friar Diego de Mercado wrote:

> *…that years ago he had held a conversation with an Otomi* [indigenous Mexican] *Indian…on matters relating to our faith. The Indian narrated to him how, long ago, the Otomis were in possession of a book handed down from father to son and guarded by persons of importance, whose duty it was to explain it. Each page of that book had…paintings which represented Christ crucified…and such is the God who reigns…the old man could not give the details, but said that, were it in existence yet, it would be evident that the teaching of that book and the preaching of the friar were one and the same.*[151]

---

149   Maarten Jansen and Gabina Aurora Pérez Jiménez. *Time and the Ancestors: Aztec and Mixtec Ritual Art*. Leiden, Netherlands; Brill Academic Pub., 2017. p. 8.

150   E. P. Grondine. *Re: The Sun of the Wind, a passage from the Historia Tolteca-Chichieca*. Forum: New World. 30 Apr 2017. <https://www.archaeologica.org/forum/search.php?keywords=precious+feathers&t=3853&sf=msgonly > Accessed 7 Feb 2019.

151   Juan Torquemada. *Monarquia Indiana*. Spain, 1723. Quoted in: P. De Roo. *History of America Before Columbus, Vol. 1, American Aborigines*. Philadelphia: J. B. Lippincott Co., 1900. pp. 424-425. <https://books.google.com/books?id=oudBAAAAIAAJ&pg=PA424&lpg=PA424&dq> 7 Sep 2018.

BEGINNING OF THE END

Toltec (Nephite) Losses

According to Bancroft, it would appear that, as a military leader, Hueman's successor, Acxitl, was not having a lot of success.

> *The* [invaders] *introduce a new divinity, and a new worship, which Acxitl, as successor of Quetzalcoatl, made a desperate effort to overthrow. He marched with all the forces he could...but was defeated in every battle. What was worse yet, during his absence on this campaign, the... invaders were admitted under their leader...into Tollan itself. Civil strife ensued in the streets of the capital between the...rival sects, until Tollan with all her noble structures, was well-nigh in ruins.*[152]

Interestingly, Bancroft refers to Acxitl as a successor of Quetzalcoatl. The name Quetzalcoatl appears to be used here as a title for their spiritual leader. Hueman may have passed the title on to his son. This would support the idea that Hueman, like Mormon, was also a spiritual leader. It also provides additional support that Acxitl, as Hueman's son, may have been their name for Moroni, Mormon's son.

Acxitl had been marching with all his forces and apparently left Tollan unguarded. The adversary may have then made an end-run around the Toltecs (Nephites), attacking the unguarded Tollan.

The Toltec (Nephites) were apparently arming themselves with obsidian arrowheads and spear points from Tollan/Teotihuacán. Following the loss of Tollan, the Toltecs (Nephites) probably lost

---

152 Bancroft. p. 280–281.

control of nearby Teotihuacán. The goal of the adversary would have been to deny the Toltecs (Nephites) the ability to arm themselves.

The loss of Tollan may have occurred about the same time that the facade of the temple in Teotihuacán was desecrated. The front of the Temple of the Feathered Serpent in Teotihuacán was:

> ...*covered by a structure called the Adosada Platform in the fourth century... This leads researches to speculate that the power shifted away from the Feathered Serpent ideology.*[153]

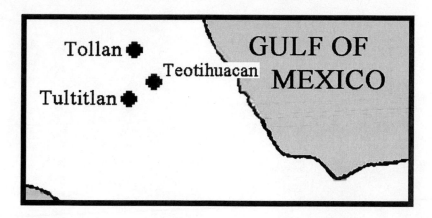

If the "Feathered Serpent ideology" in Teotihuacán represented a form of Christianity among these ancient people, this would support the idea of a Nephite worship center being desecrated by Lamanite invaders.

---

153 "The Citadel and the Feathered Serpent Pyramid." *On the Road in Teotihuacan.* <https://www.ontheroadin.com/Mexico%20Archeology/Citadel%20and%20The%20 Feathered%20Serpent%20Pyramid.htm> 17 Oct 2019.

RETURNED TO MILITARY LEADERSHIP

Mormon Comes Out of Retirement

> *And it came to pass that I* [Mormon]...*did repent of the oath which I made, that I would no more assist them* [the Nephites]; *and they gave me command again of their armies: for they looked upon me as though I could deliver them from their afflictions.*
>
> —Mormon 2:26 (5:1)

With the defeat of Tollan and Teotihuacán, the Toltecs (Nephites) lost their ability to arm themselves. This may be why Mormon regretted retiring from military leadership.

Huemac Comes Out of Retirement

Neither Bancroft nor the *Popol Vuh* mentions anything about Hueman (or Huemac) retiring. However, Bancroft did state:

> *The aged Huemac came out from his retirement and strove with the ardor of youth to ward off the destruction which he could but attribute to his indiscretions of many years ago."*[154]

After Huemac came out of retirement, he appeared to have put himself in command of a large division of the Toltec army. It was probably a shared leadership with his son, Acxitl.

---

154 Bancroft. p. 283.

Huemac/Mormon Coincidences

Mormon repented of his oath and Huemac refers to his indiscretion years before. Mormon returned to commanding his armies and Huemac came out of retirement to re-enter the battlefield. Both are saying the same thing. The similarities are so close that it is difficult to call it just a coincidence.

MAJOR LOSSES

Nephite Losses—A.D. 379–380[155]

> *But it came to pass that whatsoever lands we had passed by, and the inhabitants thereof were not gathered in, were destroyed by the Lamanites, and their towns, and villages, and cities were burned with fire; and thus the three hundred and seventy and nine years passed away. And it came to pass that in the three hundred and eightieth year, the Lamanites did come again against us to battle, and we did stand against them boldly; but it was all in vain, for so great were their numbers that they did tread the people of the Nephites under their feet. And it came to pass that we did again take to flight, and they whose flight were swifter than the Lamanites did escape, and they whose flight did not exceed the Lamanites, were swept down and destroyed.*
>
> —Mormon 2:31–33 (5:5–7)

The Nephites would never again succeed in battle. They were seriously outnumbered.

---

155   Based on the Book of Mormon 360-day vague years

Mormon was frustrated with the degree of wickedness displayed by his fellow Nephites. He was also aware that calling upon them to repent would be fruitless. He also knew that, because of the wickedness of his people, they would not bear witness of the truth of the things he had written. Mormon did not go into detail regarding the wickedness that he saw:

> …*because of the commandment which I* [Mormon] *have received, and also that ye might not have too great sorrow because of the wickedness of this people*
>
> —Mormon 2:36 (5:9).

He knew that the Lamanites would destroy the records of his people. The records would have "*to be hid up unto the Lord, that they may come forth in his own due time*" (Mormon 2:39 [5:12]). However, Mormon went on to address the people of a future generation to whom the Lord would eventually reveal his words.

> *And this is the commandment which I have received; and behold* [the things which are written] *shall come forth according to the commandment of the Lord, when he shall see fit, in his wisdom. And behold they shall go unto the unbelieving of the Jews; and for this intent shall they go: that they may be persuaded that Jesus is the Christ, the Son of the living God; that the Father may bring about, through his most beloved, his great and eternal purpose, in the restoring the Jews or all the house of Israel, to the land of their inheritance, which the Lord their God hath given them, unto the fulfilling of his covenant, and also that the*

seed of this people may more fully believe his gospel, which
shall go forth unto them from the Gentiles...

—Mormon 2:40–42 (5:13–14)

Toltec Losses

According to Bancroft, the Toltecs (Nephites) were repeatedly defeated.

At Tultitlan a final stand was made by Acxitl's orders. For many days the battle raged here until the Toltecs [Nephites] were nearly exterminated, and driven back step by step to Tollan, Xaltocan, Teotihuacán, and Xochitlalpan successively...[156]

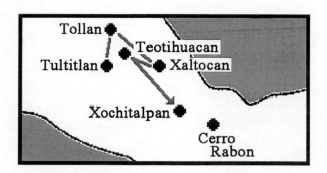

The battle at Tultitlan was probably a major attempt by the Toltecs to regain a source of weaponry.

Bancroft suggests the locations of a series of battles between the Toltecs and their foe. If Huemac's enemies had gained control of Tollan and Teotihuacán, why would Huemac or Acxitl lead his army from Xaltocan back toward the foe's center of power?

---

156   Bancroft. p. 284.

Huemac and Acxitl may have made a great show of fleeing toward Xaltocan, hoping that the enemy's army would depart out of their strongholds, Tollan and Teotihuacán, to pursue them. This would have left Tollan and Teotihuacán relatively unprotected.

As Huemac or Acxitl approached Xaltocan, another part of their army may have tried to make an end-run around the enemy to reach Teotihuacán while it was unguarded. The hope would have been that they could take and then defend the city. It would have been a chance for Huemac and Acxitl to easily arm their troops with arrowheads and spear tips while denying armament to their foe.

This tactic may seem far-fetched. However, this may have been the same tactic used by their foe that had resulted in their loss of Tollan and Teotihuacán a few years earlier.

The same tactic had been successfully used by the Nephites many years earlier. Mormon, who had been summarizing the history of his people, would have been aware of this strategy. The Book of Alma recorded a similar tactic regarding the Nephite city of Mulek [Alma 24:26–34 (52:21–26)]. It had been overtaken by a Lamanite army. In wanting to repossess the city, a portion of the Nephite army appeared to flee away from the city. The Lamanite army followed in pursuit. After they departed, another Nephite army easily retook and defended the city.

If this was Huemac's plan, the tactic did not work. They had to flee toward Xochitlalpan—much further away but closer to Cerro Rabon/Hill Cumorah.

The loss of Tollan and Teotihuacán is supported by archaeology. Spearthrower Owl is believed to have "*ascended to the throne of*

Teotihuacán on 4 May [A.D.] *374.*"[157] This date, when converted to Book of Mormon vague-years, would have been about A.D. 382. The name, Spearthrower Owl, would not have been the original name but was used by archaeologists centuries later based on the appearance of the glyph that was used to represent him.

The battles around Teotihuacán, Tollan, and Tultitlan were over. The adversary now had complete control.

Mormon's Letter to Lamanite King

Bancroft suggests Xochitlalpan as the location of the final battle. However, this may be the site from which Mormon (Hueman):

> *...wrote an epistle unto the king of the Lamanites and desired of him that he would grant unto us that we might gather together our people unto the land of Camorah, by the hill which was called Camorah* [Cerro Rabon], *and there we would give them battle. And it came to pass that the king of the Lamanites did grant unto me the thing which I desired.*
>
> —Mormon 3:3–4 (6:2–3)

The fact that Mormon wrote a letter to the king of the Lamanites and his request was granted suggests again that Mormon was still considered the primary military leader of the Nephite armies.

---

157   Derek Whaley, ed. "Spearthrower Owl, King of Teotihuacán." *Dynastology.* 9 Jun 2012. <http://dynastology.blogspot.com/2012/06/spearthrower-owl-king-of-teotihuacan.html> 16 Oct 2019.

The Cumorah Battle—A.D. 384[158]

> *And when three hundred and eighty and four years had passed away, we had gathered in all the remainder of our people unto the land Camorah.*
>
> —Mormon 3:6 (6:5)

Before passing the sacred plates to his son, Mormon wrote of that final major battle.

> *And it came to pass that they came to battle against us, and every soul was filled with terror, because of the greatness of their numbers…they did fall upon my people with the sword, and with the bow, and with the arrow, and with the axe, and with all manner of weapons of war… And when they had gone through and hewn down all my people save it were twenty and four of us, (among whom was my son Moroni,) and we having survived the dead of our people, did behold on the morrow, when the Lamanites had returned unto their camps, from the top of the Hill Camorah, the ten thousand of my people which were hewn down, being led in front by me.*
>
> —Mormon 3:10–14 (6:8–11)

Mormon went on to indicate twenty-two other leaders and their 10,000 each had all fallen. Twenty-three leaders of 10,000 each would mean 230,000 Nephites were killed. The twenty-four survivors mentioned here are all those who were able to gather together at the end of

---

158   Based on the Book of Mormon 360-day vague years

the day. It will become apparent that many escaped southward. It is also likely that more were hiding out in other places or escaped northward.

According to Bancroft,[159] Huemac was slain during this final battle. With only a few survivors and their histories past along for so many years, the foe likely believed that Huemac was among the thousands who had been slain.

MORMON'S LAST DAYS

Mormon's Final Thoughts

After describing the Cumorah battle, Mormon added a few words regarding his purpose for writing the abridgment of his people's history. In this case, he primarily addressed his thoughts to the surviving descendants of Lehi's family—the Nephites and Lamanites. He wrote to those who might survive or their descendants, hoping that they would:

> *Know ye that ye are of the house of Israel. Know ye that ye must come unto repentance, or ye cannot be saved. Know ye that ye must lay down your weapons of war, and delight no more in the shedding of blood, and take them not again, save it be that God shall command you. Know ye that ye must come to the knowledge of your fathers, and repent of all of your sins and iniquities, and believe in Jesus Christ, that he is the Son of God, and that he was slain by the Jews, and by the power of the Father he hath risen again, whereby he hath gained the victory over the grave; and also in him is the sting of death swallowed up. And he*

---

159 Bancroft. p. 284.

bringeth to pass the resurrection of the dead, whereby man
must be raised to stand before his judgment seat.

—Mormon 3:24–27 (7:2–5)

Plates to Moroni—A.D. 384[160]

Mormon probably knew his death was near. He was in his seventy-fourth year and likely experiencing the difficulties that come with age. Before that major confrontation in the land of Cumorah, Mormon wrote of giving the plates to his son, Moroni.

> *...I, Mormon, began to be old; knowing it to be the last struggle of my people, and having been commanded of the Lord that I should not suffer that the records which had been handed down by our fathers, which were sacred, to fall into the hands of the Lamanites, (for the Lamanites would destroy them,) therefore I made this record out of the plates of Nephi, and hid up in the hill of Camorah, all the records which had been entrusted to me by the hand of the Lord, save it were these few plates which I gave unto my son Moroni.*

—Mormon 3:7–8 (6:6)

After that Cumorah battle and adding his final thoughts, Mormon gave his son, *"these few plates."* More will be discussed in the next chapter regarding those plates.

Cerro Rabon/Hill Cumorah is a large limestone outcrop. It is:

---

160   Based on the Book of Mormon 360-day vague years.

...located in the Mexican state of Oaxaca, is home to some of Mexico's largest cave systems. The most impressive of these...[has been] *mapped to a length of over 24 kilometres* [15 miles] *and a depth of over 1.2 kilometres* [4,000 feet].*"*[161]

If Mormon was looking for a place to hide the remaining plates such that the Lamanites could not easily find and destroy them, such a complex cave system would have been ideal.

The remainder of the book named Mormon [chapter 4 (8–9)] was written by Mormon's son, Moroni.

AFTER CUMORAH AND MORMON'S DEATH

Mormon's Death

> *And now it came to pass that after the great and tremendous battle at Camorah, behold, the Nephites which had escaped into the country southward, were hunted by the Lamanites, until they were all destroyed; and my father was also killed by them...*
>
> —Mormon 4:1–2 (8:1–3)

Toltec's Final defeat—A.D. 386[162]

As will be seen, several major Mayan sites changed hands around A.D. 378–379. All of these sites are southward from the Hill Cumorah/Cerro Rabon. This date was based on archaeological evidence

---

161 "Cerro Rabón." *Beyond the Sump.* <https://www.beyondthesump.org/cerro-rabon> 22 Oct 2019.

162 Based on the Book of Mormon 360-day vague years

interpreted according to the standard calendar used today. This date, in Book of Mormon vague-years, would have been about A.D. 386–387. In other words, these sites appear to have changed hands at about the same time as, or shortly after, Mormon's death. It was only a few years earlier that the Toltecs (Nephites) lost control over Teotihuacán.

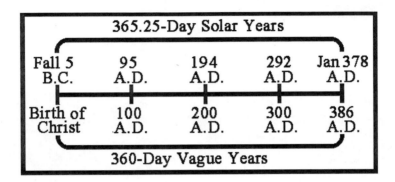

The influence of Spearthrower Owl, who conquered Teotihuacán, was now felt all the way to Tikal.[163]

In A.D. 378, a group of Teotihuacános organized a coup d'etat in Tikal, Guatemala. This was not the Teotihuacán state; it was a group of the Feathered-Serpent people thrown out from the city. The Feathered-Serpent Pyramid was burnt, all the sculptures were torn from the temple, and another platform was built to efface the facade…[164]

---

163   Zack Lindsey. "Unbounding the Past: Events in Ancient and Contemporary Maya History for May" *IMS Explorer, Institute of Maya Studies*, Vol. 47, No. 5, May 2019. p. 2.

164   Linda R. Manzanilla. "Teotihuacan: An Exceptional Multiethnic City in Pre-Hispanic Central Mexico." *Center for Latin American Studies: UC Berkeley*. 15 April 2015. <https://clas.berkeley.edu/events/spring-2015/teotihuacan-exceptional-multiethnic-city-pre-hispanic-central-mexico> 9 Aug 2018.

...a lord from Teotihuacán named...Fire is Born, arrived at Tikal: a.d. January 31, 378. It is probably no coincidence that the 14th king of Tikal...died the same day.[165]

Recall that the Feathered-Serpent Pyramid in Teotihuacán had been desecrated after the occupation by this enemy a few years earlier. Likewise, this same foe from Teotihuacán forced the Feathered-Serpent people out and desecrated their temple in Tikal. And, like Teotihuacán, a platform was built to destroy the facade. It would appear that this (Lamanite) foe was very antagonistic against the worship of this creator deity.

There may have been a few Nephites who had possibly remained behind as vassals to their Lamanite overlords during the truce. The Nephites who were fleeing from the north may have strengthened and encouraged them to join the losing rebellion against the Lamanites. Tolerating these Nephites was not an option for the Lamanites.

In 378 AD, Siyaj K'ak' (Fire is Born) of Tikal defeated Uaxactun in a war between the two cities. The two cities [Tikal and Uaxactun] joined in a combined political entity and dominated the Petén area for the next 180 years.[166]

---

165   David Roberts. "Secrets of the Maya: Deciphering Tikal." *Smithsonian.com.* Jul 2005. <https://www.smithsonianmag.com/history/secrets-of-the-maya-deciphering-ti-kal-2289808/> 16 Oct 2019.

166   "Mayan History (Part 42): Uaxactun." *Autodidact-adventures.* May 20, 2017. <https://autodidact-adventures.tumblr.com/post/160856793490/mayan-history-part-42-uaxac-tun> 19 Oct 2019.

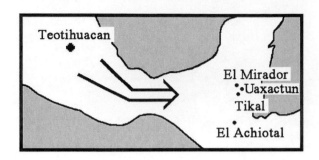

At another Mayan site, El Achiotal, a broken stone monument was found indicating that a king was celebrating forty years in power.

> *David Stuart, an epigrapher (a person who studies written inscriptions) of the University of Texas at Austin has pinpointed the date of the stela as 22 November, 418 AD. This was a period of great political upheaval in the Maya territory, primarily because a warrior-king from Teotihuacán, by the name of Siyaj K'ahk, had arrived in the area* [forty years earlier] *in 378 AD and established a new political order. The king at El Achiotal came to power shortly afterward.*[167]

Again, this A.D. 378 would be equivalent to about A.D. 386 in Book of Mormon years.

The site known as El Mirador had been in decline for several years. Nevertheless, evidence was found in El Mirador of a major battle, apparently from this same period.

> *...high on the* [Tigre] *pyramid...were found skeletons with obsidian arrow points in their ribs, possibly casualties*

167   Robin Whitlock. "Discovery of Hidden Mayan Stela and Panels Give Hints to the Importance of History in the Preclassical Period." *Ancient Origins.* 23 Jul 2015. <https://www.ancient-origins.net/news-history-archaeology/discovery-hidden-mayan-stela-and-panels-give-hints-importance-history-020453> 23 Oct 2019.

of an Early Classic period battle that wiped out remnant inhabitants of the abandoned capital.[168]

There are over 200 obsidian tips and these come from the Central Mexican highlands [Lamanite]…The chert points [Nephite] are…from the Maya area and believed to have been used by warriors from El Mirador.…The hypothesis seems to be that the people from Teotihuacán / Tikal, after the entrada in 378 decided to finish off El Mirador once and for all.[169]

Within a matter of two to three years, all these Mayan sites appear to have had a change in leadership. The depictions in the carvings and murals of these new rulers are similar to those who had recently conquered Teotihuacán. The weaponry, mentioned above, also confirms that they were from central Mexico.

Hunted from Place to Place

The end of the Toltecs (Nephites), for those who fled southward, is reflected in the archaeological record. Many years later, Moroni wrote:

Behold, four hundred years have passed away since the coming of our Lord and Saviour.…the Lamanites have hunted my people, the Nephites, down from city to city, and from place to place, even until they are no more; and

---

168   Chip Brown. "El Mirador, the Lost City of the Maya." *Smithsonian Magazine*. May 2011. <https://www.smithsonianmag.com/history/el-mirador-the-lost-city-of-the-maya-1741461/> 27 Jun 2018.

169   Johan Normark (posted by). "The Last Stand at El Mirador?" Archaeological Haecceities. 17 Sep 2009. <https://haecceities.wordpress.com/2009/09/17/the-last-stand-at-el-mirador/> 5 Jul 2018.

great has been their fall; yea, great and marvellous is the
destruction of my people, the Nephites.

—Mormon 4:7–8 (8: 6–7)

Moroni indicates that the Nephites, like the Toltecs, were hunted
"*down from city to city, and from place to place.*" Archaeology has provided a suggested list of some of those places.

CONCLUSION

When comparing the history of Hueman with the history of
Mormon, it is very likely that these are the histories of the same person. Both of them...

- lived in the area of central and southern Mexico,

- were military leaders and spiritual leaders according to their
  own people,

- were the chief leaders of one of two major groups of people,

- were associated with being exiled from their homeland,

- participated in a ten-year truce with their adversary,

- possessed the accumulated library and history of his nation,

- involved with writing the history of their people in a book that
  was considered sacred,

- that sacred book disappeared or became hidden

- retired from leading their military forces—which was later
  regretted,

- came out of retirement and returned to the battlefield after the truce expired, and

- were the leaders of a people who were hunted from place to place and destroyed.

Events described in the Book of Mormon combined with the ancient Mayan and Toltec histories and legends provide us with one compatible account. Taken together, it is easier to see Mormon as a real individual in the time and era described in the Book of Mormon. I believe the Book of Mormon is about…

REAL PEOPLE IN REAL PLACES!

CHAPTER 10:

MORONI, THOSE PLATES, AND HIS JOURNEY

Introduction

Moroni became the ultimate messenger who would deliver those recorded histories of old to Joseph Smith. Consequently, the description of Moroni's life raises some interesting questions.

- Once Moroni had the plates, what did he add? Where did he get his information?

- Some of the plates that Moroni delivered to Joseph Smith were sealed. Joseph was not allowed to translate them. Where did those sealed plates come from? What did they contain?

- For Joseph Smith to translate the plates, he initially used what was called the "interpreters." What was the source of those interpreters? How did they end up in Moroni's hands so he could pass them along?

- If all these events among the Nephites and Jaredites occurred in Mexico and Central America, how did those sacred plates and interpreters end up near Manchester, New York in the hands of Joseph Smith?

I intend to provide plausible explanations for each of these questions. Scriptural references within the Book of Mormon come into play along with trying to see Moroni as a real person who was guided by the Lord in a larger plan.

MORONI AND NEPHITE SURVIVORS

Moroni wrote:

> ...the Nephites which had escaped into the country south-ward, were hunted by the Lamanites, until they were all destroyed and my father was also killed by them.
>
> —Mormon 4:2 (8:2–3)

It is interesting to note that, according to Bancroft, after Huemac had been killed in battle, his son, "*Acxitl escaped by hiding in a cave at Xico in Lake Chalco.*"[170] That lake is northwest of Cerro Rabon. Acxitl must have fled northward. He was probably trying to return toward that area where his father had been king—Tezcuco. The cave may have been about seventeen miles SSE of Tezcuco. Because of the foe, he knew he could not go home but he could get close to that area where he was more familiar with the resources available. If Acxitl, Hueman's son, was the Mayan name for Moroni, then the statement that those Nephites who fled southward were destroyed is more easily understood. Moroni survived by escaping northward. This leaves open the idea that there were other Nephites who did not flee southward and survived. They may have hidden out and/or escaped northward.

After writing of the death of his father, Moroni wrote:

---

170   Bancroft. p. 284.

...I, even I remaineth alone to write the sad tale of the destruction of my people. But behold, they are gone, and I fulfil the commandment of my father

—Mormon 4:2–3 (8:3)

No one remained to help him write. Probably only elite members of the Nephite leadership had been schooled in reading and writing in their ancient language. Moroni is now confronted with the fact that they had all been killed and he *"remaineth alone* to write." Moroni went on to say:

...I am alone: my father hath been slain in battle, and all my kinsfolk, and I have not friends nor whither to go; and how long that the Lord will suffer that I may live, I know not.

—Mormon 4:4–6 (8:5).

He was mourning the death of his father, relatives, and friends. Anyone suffering such a loss would feel alone regardless of how many others may have survived. I believe there were other Nephite survivors besides Moroni. Small groups may have slowly, cautiously, and quietly found each other and secretly gathered for their mutual protection. Working as a small group and away from the conflict would be their only choice. The Lord must have guided them in accordance with their faith.

Only Moroni Remains with the Records

Mormon had commanded Moroni to complete the records that he had started. However, Moroni wrote:

I have but a few things to write…And behold, I would write it also, if I had room upon the plates; but I have not; and ore I have none.

—Mormon 4:1, 6 (8:1, 5)

It is interesting that after Moroni wrote about not having any ore, in the very next verse he stated that "…*four hundred years have passed away since the coming of our Lord and Saviour*" (Mormon 4:7 [8:6]). It had been about sixteen years since Moroni received the plates from his father. It would appear that during the intervening years between those two verses, he was able to procure the necessary ore and/or plates to finish his portion of the record.

Obtaining ore and making more plates would have been easier if there was a small group of Nephites surviving together. Varied talents and abilities would have allowed greater opportunities to provide for each other's needs and welfare.

THOSE FEW PLATES

Mormon gave Moroni those *few plates* (Mormon 3:8 [6:6]). Those "*few plates*" minimally included:

- Mormon's abridgment of the large plates of Nephi,
- small plates of Nephi, and
- sealed plates containing the vision of the brother of Jared and the interpreters.

These plates were eventually delivered to Joseph Smith. The idea that Mormon gave Moroni those *"few plates"* would suggest that many more plates or records would remain hidden in the Hill Cumorah.

Moroni must have also had temporary possession of Ether's twenty-four gold plates. As his father had abridged the history of the Nephites, Moroni abridged the history of the Jaredites. However, those gold plates were not among the plates that were delivered to Joseph Smith.

LARGE AND SMALL PLATES OF NEPHI

Nephi, the son of Lehi who left Jerusalem during Zedekiah's reign, was directed by the Lord to keep two sets of records. They are often referred to as the large plates of Nephi and the small plates of Nephi. Nephi, who created both sets of plates, described the purpose of each one.

> *…for the* [large] *plates upon which I make a full account of my people, I have given the name of Nephi; wherefore, they are called the plates of Nephi, after mine own name; and these* [small] *plates also, are called the plates of Nephi. Nevertheless, I have received a commandment of the Lord, that I should make these* [small] *plates, for the special purpose that there should be an account engraven of the ministry of my people. Upon the other* [large] *plates should be engraven an account of the reign of the Kings, and the wars, and contentions of my people….*
>
> —1 Nephi 2:94–97 (9:2–4)

Large Plates of Nephi

Nephi described his initial intention regarding the content of the large plates.

> *Behold I make an abridgment of the record of my father,*
> *upon plates which I have made with mine own hands;*
> *wherefore, after that I have abridged the record of my*
> *father, then will I make an account of mine own life.*
>
> —1 Nephi 1:17 (1:17)

Since the large plates were for "*the reign of the Kings, and the wars, and the contentions of my people*" (1 Nephi 2:97 [9:4]), they were subsequently passed from king to king. Each king would add an account of the people during his reign. The last king in this succession of kings was King Mosiah II.

King Mosiah II had two sons. During the latter part of his reign, neither son wanted to be king. It was then agreed that there would be no more kings among the Nephites. Instead, they would be ruled by a group of judges that would be elected by the people. The reign of judges was to begin after the death of King Mosiah (Mosiah 13:14–17 [29:11–13]).

> *Alma* [II] *was appointed to be the chief judge; he being*
> *also the high priest; his father* [Alma I] *having conferred*
> *the office upon him, and had given him the charge con-*
> *cerning all the affairs of the church.*
>
> —Mosiah 13:63 (29:42)

...king Mosiah [II]...took the plates of brass, and all the things which he had kept, and conferred them upon Alma [II]...all the records, and also the interpreters...commanding him that he should keep and preserve them, and also keep a record of the people, handing them down from one generation to another, even as they had been handed down from the time that Lehi left Jerusalem.

—Mosiah 13:1–2 (28:20)

From that time forward, it appears that the plates and sacred records were passed from spiritual leader to spiritual leader. After the accumulation of many centuries of detailed records, the volume and weight of those plates must have been considerable.

Care of all these sacred records was eventually passed from Ammaron to Mormon. It would be from the large plates of Nephi that Mormon would write an abridgment of the history of his people. That abridgment was subsequently delivered to Moroni and the large plates were left hidden in the Hill Cumorah.

Small Plates of Nephi

After Nephi had been maintaining and adding to the large plates for some time, he was commanded to also create the small plates of Nephi.

And I knew not...when I made...[the large plates], *that I should be commanded of the Lord to make these* [small] *plates... And after that I made these* [small] *plates...I, Nephi, received a commandment, that the ministry, and the prophecies, the more plain and precious parts of them, should be written upon these* [small] *plates; and that the*

things which were written, should be kept for the instruc-
tion of my people, which should possess the land, and also
for other wise purposes, which purposes, are known unto
the Lord... And this I have done, and commanded my
people that they should do, after that I was gone, and that
these plates should be handed down from one generation
to another, or from one prophet to another, until further
commandments of the Lord.

—1 Nephi 5:220, 222–226 (19:2–4)

Both the large and small plates of Nephi were to be passed from generation to generation. While the large plates were initially passed from king to king, the small plates were passed from spiritual leader to spiritual leader. Each generation was charged with adding to that record. After several generations, Amaleki was in possession of the small plates of Nephi.

And it came to pass that I [Amaleki] *began to be old; and,*
having no seed, and knowing king Benjamin to be a just
man before the Lord, wherefore, I shall deliver up these
plates unto him, exhorting all men to come unto God, the
Holy One of Israel...

—Omni 1:43 (1:25)

Passed Along

King Benjamin, the father of Mosiah II, already possessed the large plates of Nephi. After that time, there would be no more additions to the small plates of Nephi. The small plates were simply passed along with all the other sacred records. Many centuries later, Mormon explained his inclusion of the small plates with his abridgment.

> *I searched among the records which had been delivered into my hands, and I found these plates. which contained this small account of the Prophets, from Jacob, down to the reign of this king Benjamin; and also many of the words of Nephi. And the things which are upon these plates pleasing me, because of the prophecies of the coming of Christ; and my fathers knowing that many of them have been fulfilled...wherefore, I chose these things, to finish my record upon them, which remainder of my record I shall take from the* [large] *plates of Nephi...I shall take these* [small] *plates, which contain these prophecyings and revelations, and put them with the remainder of my* record [abridgment of the large plates], *for they are choice unto me; and I know they will be choice unto my brethren. And I do this for a wise purpose; for thus it whispereth me, according to the workings of the spirit of the Lord which is in me.*
>
> —Words of Mormon 1:5–10 (1:3–7)

Mormon had been working on his summary of the large plates of Nephi. He had completed that portion beginning with Lehi down to the time of King Benjamin. The small plates of Nephi covered the same period. However, the difference in emphasis intrigued Mormon. He then added the small plates, unchanged, into his record. It was

Mormon's way of finishing his "*record upon them,*" referring to the time from Lehi to King Benjamin.

Interestingly, Nephi had started the small plates "*for other wise purposes...known unto the Lord*" (1 Nephi 5:224 [19:3]). Almost a thousand years later, Mormon inserted th*em into his abridgment "for a wise purpose...according to the workings of the spirit of the Lord"* (Words of Mormon 1:10 [1:7]).

The Lord's Purpose for the Small Plates

Many centuries later, Joseph Smith began translating the plates that were delivered to him by Moroni. Martin Harris became a scribe for Joseph Smith during the early days of the translation process. After "*two intensive months as Joseph Smith's scribe in the summer of 1828...* [he] *produced 116 manuscript pages....*"[171] Martin Harris then prevailed upon Joseph Smith to loan him those pages to show his friends. Despite warnings from the Lord, Joseph loaned the manuscript to Martin. The manuscript was subsequently lost or stolen. As a result, the plates and interpreters were taken away from Joseph Smith by an Angel. About five months later, the plates were returned. Joseph Smith was told not to retranslate the lost portion nor was Martin Harris allowed to be his scribe.

Joseph Smith subsequently renewed his efforts at translating the Book of Mormon beginning with the small plates of Nephi.[172] The small plates covered the same time frame as the lost portion with

---

171   Richard Anderson. *Investigating the Book of Mormon Witnesses.* Salt Lake City, UT: Deseret Book Co., 1981. p. 6.

172   My focus here is on the life of Moroni and the importance of the small plates of Nephi. Much has already been published by both the RLDS and LDS denominations regarding Joseph Smith and the translation process.

greater emphasis on the spiritual aspects and fewer details about the wars and atrocities that had been committed. One unique aspect of the small plates is that they were not an abridgment. They were the actual writings of multiple authors. Each had added to the plates before they were passed along.

From the small plates of Nephi, we now have the first six books in the Book of Mormon: 1 Nephi, 2 Nephi, Jacob, Enos, Jarom, and Omni. This is followed by the Words of Mormon (quoted above) in which Mormon described finding the small plates of Nephi and his reason for including them with his abridgment of the large plates. The record then continued with Mormon's abridgment of the large plates of Nephi which provides us with the next five books in the Book of Mormon: Mosiah, Alma, Helaman, 3 Nephi, 4 Nephi. This is followed by Mormon's personal observations and the contributions of his son, Moroni.

TWENTY-FOUR GOLD PLATES

Ether's Gold Plates Passed Along

Ether, the last Jaredite prophet, wrote a summary of the history of his people. It was engraved on twenty-four gold plates.[173] Eventually, the plates were delivered to King Mosiah II who was able to provide a translation by using the interpreters, which will be discussed later. From that time on, it appears that possession of Ether's plates was passed from generation to generation along with the large and small plates of Nephi.

---

173   The discovery of those plates was described in Chapter 5, Zeniff's Colony.

Alma's Advice

Several years after Mosiah's death, Alma II spoke to each of his sons. He was seeking their help as both missionaries and military leaders to defend the people from the Lamanite aggression. Alma II told his son, Helaman:

> *...those twenty-four plates, that ye keep them, that the mysteries and the works of darkness, and their secret works, or the secret works of those people, which have been destroyed, may be made manifest unto this people; yea, all their murders, and robbings, and their plunderings, and all their wickedness, and abominations, may be made manifest unto this people....—Therefore, ye shall keep these secret plans of their oaths and their covenants from this people, and only their wickedness, and their murders, and their abominations, shall ye make known unto them...*
>
> —Alma 17:52–53, 61 (37:21, 29)

"*Those twenty-four plates*" must be a reference to Ether's writings.

Alma advised his son to tell the people of the wickedness, murders, robbings, and abominations that destroyed the Jaredites. However, he did not want Helaman to be specific about their secret oaths and covenants for fear that others would imitate them.

Moroni Summarizes Ether's Record

After Moroni finished his father's portion of the record [Mormon chapter 4 (chapters 8–9)], he added a summary of the history of the Jaredites. He introduced the Book of Ether with the following:

And now I, Moroni, proceed to give an account of those ancient inhabitants which were destroyed by the hand of the Lord upon the face of this north country. And I take mine account from the twenty and four plates which were found by the people of Limhi, which is called the Book of Ether.

—Ether 1:1–2 (1:1–2)

It appears that Moroni had the original twenty-four gold plates in his possession. Like Mosiah, Moroni must have used the interpreters to be able to read the plates.

Moroni's reference to "*this north country*" suggests that he was still in his home territory. This would place him in Mexico, north of the Isthmus of Tehuantepec, and perhaps close to the Hill Cumorah/Cerro Rabon.

As Moroni worked on the Book of Ether, he said he was writing: "*the words which was commanded me, according to my memory*" (Ether 2:1 [5:1]). For Moroni, it was a matter of summarizing or abridging that history. However, there had to be an emphasis on those things commanded by the Lord. Moroni described his initial approach to abridging these twenty-four gold plates.

...the first part of this record, which speaketh concerning the creation of the world, and also of Adam, an account from that time even to the great tower, and whatsoever things transpired among the children of men until that time, is had among the Jews, therefore I do not write those things which transpired from the days of Adam until that time...

—Ether 1:3–4 (1:3–4)

After all these years, one might wonder how Moroni knew what was *"had among the Jews"*? Among the records that had been passed along for centuries were the brass plates. Lehi and his sons had brought that record of the Jews with them from Jerusalem. Several centuries later, the Mulekites were discovered by the people of King Mosiah I. The Mulekites (people of Zarahemla) had an oral history of their origin in Jerusalem but no written history. When they were discovered by the Nephites, the Mulekites:

> ...*did rejoice exceedingly, because that the Lord had sent the people of Mosiah* [I] *with the plates of brass which contained the record of the Jews.*

> —Omni 1:25 (1:14)

This *"record of the Jews"* was among those records that were being passed from one generation to the next along with the large and small plates of Nephi. As a spiritual leader, Moroni would have been well aware of what was recorded on those plates of brass.

Ether's gold plates began with the creation and the story of Adam. Since that was already part of Jewish sacred writings, Moroni saw no reason to repeat it. Therefore, he began his abridgment with the great tower, the confusion of tongues, and the events surrounding the brother of Jared. In other words, he began at that point where those stories available among the Jews and the history of the Jaredites diverged.

Following Alma's Advice

When Moroni summarized the Book of Ether, he wrote about secret societies and secret combinations. He wrote about one particular group of Jaredites who were led by a man named Akish.

> [Akish]…*formed a secret combination, even as they of old; which combination is most abominable and wicked above all, in the sight of God: for the Lord worketh not in secret combinations, neither doth he will that man should shed blood, but in all things hath forbidden it, from the beginning of man. And now I, Moroni, do not write the manner of their oaths and combinations…*
>
> —Ether 3:92–94 (8:18–20)

While summarizing the information from Ether's plates, Moroni appears to have followed the same inspired advice that was given by Alma to Helaman. The goal was to warn people about the evils of "*secret combinations*" and the shedding blood. However, Moroni did not give specific details regarding their "*oaths and combinations.*" Moroni went on to say that "*whatsoever nation shall uphold such secret combinations, to get power and gain, until they shall spread over the nation, behold, they shall be destroyed*" (Ether 3:95 [8:22]).

Where Are the Twenty-Four Gold Plates?

Mormon had hidden all the plates in the Hill Cumorah except those that he gave to Moroni. It appears that Ether's twenty-four gold plates were available to Moroni; however, there is no indication that they were among those plates that Moroni delivered to Joseph Smith. After recording an abridgment of Ether's record, it is possible that Moroni, himself, placed them with the other records in the Hill Cumorah. As noted above, Moroni was probably still in the area.

THE SEALED PLATES AND INTERPRETERS

Joseph Smith initially used the interpreters to translate about one-fourth of the plates delivered to him by Moroni. Some of those plates were sealed. What was the origin of those sealed plates and the interpreters? What was in those sealed plates?

Source of the Interpreters

After the brother of Jared departed from the Great Tower at the time of the confusion of tongues, he had a very powerful spiritual experience. Immediately before he experienced a promised vision, the Lord told him:

> ...behold, these two stones will I give unto thee, and ye shall seal them up also with the things which ye shall write. For behold, the language which ye shall write, I have confounded; wherefore I will cause in mine own due time that these stones shall magnify to the eyes of men, these things which ye shall write....
>
> —Ether 1:88–89 (3:23–24)

"These two stones" would "magnify to the eyes of men" the language that the Lord had "confounded." In other words, they would eventually be used to translate unknown languages. In that manner, they became known as interpreters.[174]

---

174 Three years after the Book of Mormon was published, W. W. Phelps implied that the interpreters were "known, perhaps in ancient days as...Urim and Thummim." (W. W. Phelps, ed. The Evening and Morning Star, Vol. 1, No. 8. Independence, MO, W. W. Phelps & Co.: Jan 1833.) Subsequently, varying references have referred to the Interpreters as the Urim and Thummim. Some have then suggested that this was the same Urim and Thummim mentioned in the Bible. However, time, distance, and purpose indicate otherwise.

Contents of the Sealed Plates

Soon afterward, the brother of Jared had a vision.

> ...the Lord shewed unto the brother of Jared all the inhab-
> itants of the earth which had been, and also all that would
> be; and the Lord withheld them not from his sight, even
> unto the ends of the earth.... And the Lord commanded
> the brother of Jared to go down out of the mount from
> the presence of the Lord, and write the things which he
> had seen: and they were forbidden to come unto the chil-
> dren of men, until after that he should be lifted up upon
> the cross...
>
> —Ether 1:90, 94 (3:25, 4:1)

The things that the brother of Jared wrote are contained in what became known as the sealed plates. The sealed plates and interpreter stones were to be sealed and passed along together. At some point in time, for convenience and protection, the stones were mounted on a bow and attached to a breastplate.

Passed to Mulekites

Beginning with the brother of Jared, the interpreters and sealed plates were probably passed from one Jaredite king to another. The more righteous kings could use the interpreters as intended by the Lord while it was known that the sealed plates had to remain sealed. The less righteous kings may have seen them as symbols of power and lead-ership. Possession of those things may have been used to identify the owner as the king in the same way that possession of a king's crown in some cultures could be used to identify a king. Coriantumr was the last surviving king of the Jaredites. He may have had the sealed plates and interpreters in his possession when he went to live with the Mulekites during his final days. This may be when they were passed to the Mulekite king.

It has been suggested that Ether may have passed the sealed plates and interpreters to the Mulekites. However, while the Mulekites recalled Coriantumr. there is no record of any contact with Ether.

Later, when the Nephites first encountered the Mulekites, the Mulekites must have had the sealed plates and interpreters already in their possession. Since the Mulekites "*had brought no records with them*" (Omni 1:30 [1:17]) and lacked any written records, there is no clear explanation of how they came to possess them. Yet somehow, the interpreters must have passed from the Jaredites through the hands of the Mulekites for them to end up in the hands of Mosiah I. This would have been years before King Limhi's search party found Ether's twenty-four plates of gold.

Passed to Nephites

Sometime around 200 B.C., the Mulekites accepted Nephite leadership and Mosiah I was declared their king. As such, the interpreters and sealed plates would have been passed to him. This King Mosiah I was the father of King Benjamin and the grandfather of King Mosiah II. This sacred treasure would have been passed along this line of succession.

> *And it came to pass in the days of Mosiah [I], there was a large stone brought unto him, with engravings on it; and he did interpret the engravings, by the gift and power of God. And they gave an account of one Coriantumr, and the slain of his people. And Coriantumr was discovered by*

the people of Zarahemla; and he dwelt with them for the
space of nine Moons.

—Omni 1:35–39 (1:20–22)

"*By the gift and power of God*" is the same phrase used by Joseph Smith and the three witnesses when they described the method used by Joseph Smith to translate the first part of the plates that were provided to him by Moroni. This is evidence that King Mosiah I had the interpreters.

King Benjamin is also associated with the possession of the interpreters.[175]

> *...and for this cause did king Benjamin keep them* [the sealed plates and interpreters], *that they should not come unto the world until after Christ should shew himself unto his people*
>
> —Ether 1:95 (4:1)

Recall King Limhi and his people were led by Ammon down to the land of Zarahemla. Those twenty-four gold plates left by Ether were then delivered to King Mosiah II. The people were anxious to hear the translation.

> *And now he translated them by the means of those two stones which was fastened into the rims of a bow. Now these things was prepared from the beginning, and was handed down from generation to generation, for the purpose of interpreting languages; and they have been kept*

---

175   This is also noted earlier in "Chapter 5: Zeniff's Colony."

and preserved by the hand of the Lord…and whosoever
has these things, is called seer, after the manner of old times.

—Mosiah 12:18–21 (28:13–16)

It is obvious here that king Benjamin had passed those two stones or interpreters to his son, Mosiah. He then used the interpreters to translate Ether's plates. However, the sealed plates were not to be translated—yet.

…king Mosiah [II]…took the plates of brass, and all the
things which he had kept, and conferred them upon Alma
[II]…also the interpreters, and conferred them upon
him…

—Mosiah 13:1–2 (28:20)

After the death of King Mosiah II, the sealed plates and interpreters, along with all the other sacred records, were passed from spiritual leader to spiritual leader.

Sealed Plates Sealed Again

After Christ had appeared to the people in the Land Bountiful, "*he commanded that they* [the vision of the brother of Jared] *should be made manifest*" (Ether 1:96 [4:2]).

When Mormon passed those few plates to his son, Moroni, he must have also passed both the sealed plates and interpreters to him. The contents of the sealed plates which had been made manifest at Christ's command must now be sealed again.

And now, after that, they have all dwindled in unbelief, and there is none, save it be the Lamanites, and they have rejected the Gospel of Christ; therefore I am commanded that I should hide [the vision of the brother of Jared] *up again in the earth.*

—Ether 1:97 (4:3)

The Nephite culture came to an end because they had *"dwindled in unbelief."* Moroni then wrote:

Behold, I have written upon these plates the very things which the brother of Jared saw; and there never was greater things made manifest, than that which was made manifest unto the brother of Jared; wherefore, the Lord hath commanded me to write them; and I have wrote them. And he commanded me that I should seal them up; and he also hath commanded that I should seal up the interpretation thereof; wherefore I have sealed up the interpreters. according to the commandments of the Lord. For the Lord saith unto me, They shall not go forth unto the Gentiles until the day that they shall repent of their iniquity, and become clean before the Lord...

—Ether 1:98–100 (4:4–6)

Moroni wrote, *"upon these plates the very things which the brother of Jared saw."* That would mean that he read, translated, and included that translation with the plates that he was preparing. However, as commanded by the Lord, he sealed them up (the brother of Jared's original plates) and he also sealed up the interpretation (Moroni's translation). The interpreters were then sealed together with them. The sealed portion of the plates that Joseph Smith received may have then included both the original sealed plates and Moroni's translation.

> *And now I, Moroni...have told you the things which I have sealed up; therefore touch them not, in order that ye may translate: for that thing is forbidden you, except by and by it shall be wisdom in God.*

> —Ether 2:1 (5:1)

Joseph Smith was not allowed to translate the sealed portion of the plates that were delivered to him.

THE BOOK OF MORONI

Moroni then wrote the final book—the Book of Moroni. He wrote of the practices of the church in his day and the things taught to him by his father along with some final thoughts. He also included copies of three letters that had been written to him by his father, Mormon, before he was killed.

Moroni's Final Thoughts

> *Now I, Moroni, write somewhat as seemeth me good; and I write unto my brethren, the Lamanites; and I would that they should know that more than four hundred and twenty years has passed away, since the sign was given of the coming of Christ. And I seal up these records after that I have spoken a few words by way of exhortation unto you. Behold, I would exhort you that when ye shall read these things, if it be wisdom in God that ye should read them, that ye would remember how merciful the Lord hath been*

unto the children of men, from the creation of Adam, even down until the time that ye shall receive these things, and ponder it in your hearts. And when ye shall receive these things, I would exhort you that ye would ask God, the Eternal Father, in the name of Christ, if these things are not true; and if ye shall ask with a sincere heart, with real intent, having faith in Christ, and he will manifest the truth in you, by the power of the Holy Ghost; and by the power of the Holy Ghost, ye may know the truth of all things.

—Moroni 10:1–5 (10:1–5)

It is now A.D. 420 (Book of Mormon vague years). Moroni is writing about sealing all of the records. This suggests to me that he was in the vicinity of that hill in New York State where the records would remain hidden until that day when Joseph Smith would be guided to the location.

And I exhort you to remember these things: for the time speedily cometh that ye shall know that I lie not, for ye shall see me at the bar of God: and the Lord God will say unto you, Did I not declare my words unto you, which was written by this man, like as one crying from the dead? yea, even as one speaking out of the dust, I declare these things unto the fulfilling of the prophecies. And behold, they shall proceed forth out of the mouth of the everlasting God; and his word shall hiss forth from generation to generation. And God shall shew unto you, that that which I have written, is true.

—Moroni 10:22–26 (10:27–29)

The concept of "*one speaking out of the dust*" suggests a book that was hidden in the earth, brought forth, and translated. This was a prophecy of the eventual coming forth of the Book of Mormon. Another prophecy of this same event is also found elsewhere in the book of Mormon. Many centuries earlier, Nephi wrote:

> *After that my seed and the seed of my brethren shall have dwindled in unbelief, and shall have been smitten by the Gentiles…and after that they shall have been brought down low into the dust, even that they are not, yet the words of the righteous shall be written, and the prayers of the faithful shall be heard, and all they which have dwindled in unbelief, shall not be forgotten; for they which shall be destroyed shall speak unto them out of the ground, and their speech shall be low out of the dust, and their voice shall be as one that hath a familiar spirit; for the Lord God will give unto him power, that he may whisper concerning them, even as it were out of the ground; and their speech shall whisper out of the dust. For thus saith the Lord God: They shall write the things which shall be done among them, and they shall be written and sealed up in a book, and they that have dwindled in unbelief, shall not have them, for they seek to destroy the things of God…*
>
> —2 Nephi 11:81–86 (26:15–17)

I believe Moroni was fully aware that the record on these plates would eventually come forth in fulfillment of this prophecy.

HIDING THE PLATES

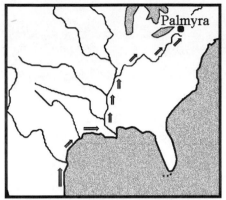

Suggested route of Moroni to the place where he buried the plates.

Moroni took the plates with him when he left his homeland following years of persecution and the destruction of his people. His long migration, probably directed by the Lord, took him to northeastern North America, probably along with a few remaining survivors. He could easily have followed the Gulf Coast and then north along the Mississippi River. The final leg would have been to the northeast by following the Ohio River. On a hill in New York State, Moroni carefully hid the plates and interpreters in a stone box. He then placed a large ordinary stone on top of it to make the hiding place inconspicuous.

Micmac Indians and Egyptian Glyphs

I believe that Moroni did not travel alone. Even though he had lost his family and friends, a small number of Nephites were probably able to quietly and secretly gather for this migration northward—far from the Lamanite animosities.

Moroni wrote: *"we have written this record according to our knowledge in the characters, which are called among us the reformed*

Egyptian…" (Mormon 4:98 [9:32]). As this group traveled together, Moroni may have taught his companions how to read and write in this ancient language.

After hiding the plates in that hill in New York, this group or their descendants may have migrated even further north and east. Some may have finally settled in the area of New Brunswick and Nova Scotia. Their descendants may have become known as the Micmac Indians.

The interesting correlation is in the fact that this Indian tribe had an established writing system long before they were discovered by the Europeans.

> *Father Le Clerq, a Roman Catholic Missionary from the late 1600s, claimed to have seen Mi'kmaq (Micmac*) children taking notes (writing) on birchbark as he was giving his lessons. Pierre Milliard, also a Catholic Priest but in 1730s, documented the Mi'kmaq writing system and claims to have added to it to help his converts learn prayers and responses to the Catholic Mass. In the interim, the birch scrolls containing the writings of past generations had been destroyed. So it is Abbe Milliard's works, including his book Manuel Hieroglyphique Micmac, that is most helpful in documenting the similarity between Mi'kmaq writing and ancient Egyptian Hieroglyphics.*[176]

---

176 Patricia Glacquinta, Ph.D. "Did the Mi'kmaq From Eastern Canada Write in Egyptian Hieroglyphics?" *Knitting It Together, Lost History, Mystery, and Yarns.* 5 Nov 2015. <https://knittingittogether.com/2016/01/20/> 26 Jun 2019.

"…many symbols in this [Micmac] *writing system resemble so strongly the sacred hieroglyphs of ancient Egypt…."*[177] The similarities between both of these ancient writing systems with parallel meanings defy explanation. This is especially significant since the Egyptian glyphs were not translated until almost a century later!

After diligent research and multiple comparisons between the Micmac glyphs and Egyptian glyphs, Barry Fell stated that it *"was now quite obvious, the Micmac writing system…is derived from ancient Egypt."*[178]

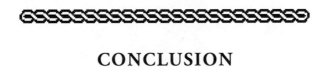

CONCLUSION

Moroni's life was caught up in some very difficult circumstances.

- He was the final custodian of the record abridged by his father.

- He had to endure the loss of family and friends.

- He finished the records provided to him according to the wishes of his father and the commandments of the Lord.

- He carried the finished plates and interpreters several thousand miles to New York State.

There is very little in the way of archaeological or legendary evidence regarding the life of Moroni except what is recorded in the

---

177 David Warner Mathisen. *The Case of the Micmac Hieroglyphs: a Powerful Blow to Isolationist Theories.* The Mathisen Corollary. 13 Jul 2011. <http://mathisencorollary. blogspot.com/2011/07/case-of-micmac-hieroglyphs-powerful.html> 23 Jun 2019.

178 Barry Fell. *America B.C., Ancient Settlers in the New World.* New York: Pocket Books, 1976. p. 257.

Book of Mormon. What I have presented is an attempt to see him as very human: enduring much, accomplishing much, and being guided by the Lord. There is also an attempt to understand more about the plates that were eventually delivered to Joseph Smith. I would only ask that each reader would consider the events described in the Book of Mormon along with the powerful testimonies of their spiritual leaders. I believe the Book of Mormon is about...

REAL PEOPLE IN REAL PLACES!

EPILOGUE

Many stories have been told and books published regarding the coming forth of the Book of Mormon. This book has been an effort to connect the events described within the Book of Mormon with ancient history, archaeology, geography, geology, and oceanography. It has been an attempt to see the people described as real people in the time and places in which they lived.

As I come to the end of my book, there are two more areas that I believe are important supplements to understanding and validating this book.

THE LANGUAGE OF THE BOOK OF MORMON

The language in the Book of Mormon has been an enigma for many years. However, time has proven that the language, writing style, and grammar are a reflection of the time and culture in which the original records were written. What follows are a few examples.

"And It Came To Pass"; "And Thus It Is"

"And it came to pass" is probably the most frequently used phrase in the Book of Mormon. This phrase in the idiom of King James English is a rendering of the Hebrew word "vayehee." Its frequent use in the Book of Mormon is consistent with the frequent use of "vayehee" in the Old Testament Hebrew text…. This phrase, "and it came to

pass" and the frequent use of "and" are two of the most important proofs of Hebrew language structure found in the Book of Mormon.[179]

What may seem to be poor English grammar, especially in its constant repetitiveness, is actually good Hebrew grammar. *"The original Hebrew (and Aramaic) manuscripts were written without vowels and without punctuation."*[180] As a result, the beginning of a new sentence or new thought was frequently identified by using the words "*and*," "*and thus it is*," and "*and it came to pass.*" This was especially true when describing a sequence of events.

In the translation of Mayan glyphs, a "*common glyph, which told of time passing and was used throughout many of the stories written by the Maya, was the date indicator 'utchi,' meaning 'And then it came to pass.'*"[181] This strongly suggests a Hebrew influence!

Items in a Series Connected with "and"

> *One prominent peculiarity of biblical Hebrew is the frequent use of the conjunction and, both in beginning a sentence and in the listing of a series within a sentence... In Hebrew when several nouns are joined by and, the possessive pronoun must be repeated with each.*[182]

---

179   Angela Crowell. "Hebraisms in the Book of Mormon." *Recent Book of Mormon Developments: Articles from The Zarahemla Record.* Independence, MO; Zarahemla Research Foundation, 1984. p. 56.

180   Ben Shaw. "Punctuating the Bible." *The Aquila Report.* 1 Nov 2011. <https://www.theaquilareport.com/punctuating-the-bible/> 26 Oct 2019.

181   Mark F. Cheney. *Mark of the Jaguar, A Book of Mormon Adventure in the Land of the Maya.* Bloomington, IN, Author House, 2014. p. 12.

182   Crowell. pp. 55–56.

Connecting nouns in a series by the repetitive "and" along with any associated pronoun was a grammatical necessity. A few examples follow from the Bible and the Book of Mormon.

> [Lehi] *was a visionary man, and that he had led them out of the land of Jerusalem, to leave the land of their inheritance, and their gold, and their silver, and their precious things, and to perish in the wilderness.*
>
> —1 Nephi 1:38 (2:111)

> *And it came to pass that the people of Nephi did till the land, and raise all manner of grain, and of fruit, and flocks of herds, and flocks of all manner of cattle, of every kind, and goats, and wild goats, and also much horses.*
>
> —Enos 1:34 (1:21)

> *people of the church began to wax proud, because of their exceeding riches, and their fine silks, and their fine twined linen, and because of many flocks and herds, and their gold, and their silver, and all manner of precious things, which they had obtained by their industry...*
>
> —Alma 2:8–9 (4:6)

> *...thou, and thy children, and thy children's children, and thy flocks, and thy herds and all that thou hast...*
>
> —Genesis 45:10, KJV)

Jacob their father, and their little ones, and their wives…
and they took their cattle, and their goods…

—Genesis 46:5–6, KJV)

Chiasmus

The chiastic structure is a form of ancient Hebrew poetry. It is a series of statements in which the latter half restates the ideas of the first half—in reverse order. The sequence might appear as A, B, C, B', A'. The central statement may even repeat as A, B, C, C', B', A'. **The central statement is the important focal point of the message**. It was not fully appreciated until the twentieth century—long after the Book of Mormon was published. The subsequent discovery of this style of Hebrew writing explains frequently repeated words or phrases in many relatively short passages in both the Bible and the Book of Mormon.

Many examples from the Book of Mormon have been previously published. However, there is one chiasm that I have not seen published. It will serve as an example of this unique form of poetry. The following is from Jacob 2:32–43 (2:23–33).

A. committing whoredoms…concerning David, and Solomon
  B. I have led this people out of the land of Jerusalem
    C. I, the Lord God will not suffer
      D. whoredoms is an abomination before me
        E. saith the Lord of Hosts
          F. this people shall keep my commandments
        E'. saith the Lord of Hosts
      D'. wickedness and abominations
    C'. I will not suffer, saith the Lord of Hosts
  B'. this people which I have led out of the land of Jerusalem
A'. they shall not commit whoredoms like unto they of old.

Final Thoughts on the Grammar

The Hebrew literary style and grammar, evident in the 1830 edition of the Book of Mormon, must have appeared awkward to Joseph Smith Jr. As a result, in 1837, a second edition was published. *"For this* [1837] *edition, hundreds of grammatical changes and a few emendations were made in the text."*[183] Joseph Smith, Jr. neither understood nor appreciated these ancient Hebrew writing styles. As a result, I can only conclude that the grammar exhibited in the original 1830 edition of the Book of Mormon is the result of a correct translation of an ancient record.

THE WITNESSES

During most of the translation process, no one except Joseph Smith was allowed to see the plates. However, the Lord did call upon two groups of people to be witnesses of the plates. Their testimonies have been included in every published copy of the Book of Mormon.

The Three Witnesses

As the translation of the Book of Mormon progressed, the following scripture was encountered in the Book of Ether. It appears to be addressed to Joseph Smith. Moroni wrote:

> *And behold, ye may be privileged that ye may shew the plates unto those who shall assist to bring forth this work; and unto three shall they be shewn by the power of God; wherefore, they shall know of a surety that these things are*

---

183 Daniel H. Ludlow, ed. "Book of Mormon Editions (1830–1981)" *Encyclopedia of Mormonism.* New York, Macmillan Publishing Co. Copyright, Brigham Young University, 1992. p. 75.

true. And in the mouth of three witnesses shall these things
be established…

—Ether 2:1–3 (5:1–4)

Immediately after this portion was translated, three people immediately volunteered. All had been involved in the translation process but had not been allowed to see the plates. After their experience, Oliver Cowdery, Martin Harris, and David Whitmer signed a document which stated in part:

> *…we declare with words of soberness, that an Angel of*
> *God came down from heaven, and he brought and laid*
> *before our eyes, that we beheld and saw the plates, and the*
> *engravings thereon; and we know that it is by the grace of*
> *God the Father, and our Lord Jesus Christ, that we beheld*
> *and bear record that these things are true…*

—1830 edition Book of Mormon

The Eight Witnesses

The second group of witnesses, Christian Whitmer, Peter Whitmer Jr., Jacob Whitmer, John Whitmer, Hiram Page, Hyrum Smith, Joseph Smith, Sr., and Samuel Smith signed a document which stated in part:

> *…Joseph Smith, Jun., the Author and Proprietor of this*
> *work, has shewn unto us the plates of which hath been spo-*
> *ken, which have the appearance of gold; and as many of*
> *the leaves as the said Smith has translated, we did handle*
> *with our hands; and we also saw the engravings thereon…*

—1830 edition Book of Mormon

Real and Sacred Plates

The three witnesses were shown the plates by an angel but did not physically touch them. The eight witnesses were shown the plates by Joseph Smith. They were able to physically handle them and turn the pages. When taken together, the emphasis is on both the reality and the sacred nature of the plates. The only witness during both occasions was Joseph Smith Jr.

Although some of these witnesses eventually left the church, none ever denied their testimony of the Book of Mormon.

CONCLUSION

Many books have already been written, both supporting the Book of Mormon and condemning it. I am aware that much of what I have written includes a lot of conjecture. However, there are a lot of "coincidences" that tie it all together. I have tried to envision these people, in their time and culture, living out the history described in the Book of Mormon. I know that there will be those who will disagree with varying aspects of what I have written. I would only ask that the coincidences in these stories that are based on documentable supporting evidence be sincerely considered.

Over the years, many have experienced personal testimonies supporting the validity of the Book of Mormon. For me, writing this book has been a very rewarding and spiritual journey of discovery.

Is the Book of Mormon true? The Lord has promised all people who will diligently and prayerfully seek the answer to this question will know the truth.

> *Ask, and it will be given you; search, and you will find; knock, and the door will be opened for you. For everyone who asks receives, and everyone who searches finds, and for everyone who knocks, the door will be opened.*
>
> —Matthew 7:7–8, NRSV

> *And God shall shew unto you, that that which I have written, is true.*
>
> —Moroni 10:26 (10:29)

I have tried to show that the events described in the Book of Mormon actually occurred. The leaders diligently recorded their testimonies of a living Christ. I believe that the events described in the Book of Mormon were written by and about…

REAL PEOPLE IN REAL PLACES!

WORKS CITED

Adela. "Quetzalcóatl Meso-American God." *Naked History.* 21 Dec 2015. <http://www.historynaked.com/quetzalcoatl-meso-american-god/> 30 Nov 2019.

Amundsen, Barry. *Phoenix, Phoenicians, Tyre and Sidon today and destiny, (remembering David Flynn).* 11 Apr 2012. <http://www.fivedoves.com/letters/apr2012/barrya411-2.htm> 22 Feb 2020.

"Ancient Egypt." *The World's Largest Online Tattoo Museum.* <http://www.vanishingtattoo.com/tattoo_museum/egyptian_tattoos.html> 28 Sep 2019.

"Arabian Camel" *NationalGeographic.com.* <https://www.nationalgeographic.com/animals/mammals/a/arabian-camel/> 23 Nov 2019.

Anderson, Richard. *Investigating the Book of Mormon Witnesses.* Salt Lake City, UT: Deseret Book Co., 1981.

Ashe, G., et al. *The Quest for America.* New York: Praeger Publishers, 1971.

Ball, Jessica. "Types of Volcanic Eruptions" Geology.com <https://geology.com/volcanoes/types-of-volcanic-eruptions/> 9 Oct 2019.

Bancroft, Hubert H. *The Works of Hubert Howe Bancroft,* Vol.V, *The Native Races, Primitive History.* San Francisco, CA: A. L. Bancroft & Co., Publishers. 1883.

Brava, Edwardo Corvantes. "United States Citizens Assure that the Hill Rabon Contains Sacred Maya Writings." *Tuxtepec, Mexico newspaper* [English translation]. 12 Apr 2005. <http://www.freerepublic.com/focus/religion/2522214/replies?c=951> 20 Oct 2019.

Brodwin, Eric. "Mexico is in the worst possible place for earthquakes—here's why it keeps getting hit." *Business Insider.* 16 Feb 2018. <https://www.businessinsider.com/why-mexico-earthquakes-science-2018-2> 5 Oct 2019.

Brown, Chip. "El Mirador, the Lost City of the Maya." *Smithsonian Magazine.* May 2011. <https://www.smithsonianmag.com/history/el-mirador-the-lost-city-of-the-maya-1741461/> 27 Jun 2018.

Brown, S. Kent. "New Light—'The Place That Was Called Nahom': New Light from Ancient Yemen." *Journal of Book of Mormon Studies,* Vol. 8, no. 1, 1999.

Butterworth, F. Edward. *Pilgrims of the Pacific.* Independence, MO: Herald House, 1974.

Cartwright, Mark. "Olmec Civilization." *Ancient History Encyclopedia.* 4 Apr 2018. <https://www.ancient.eu/Olmec_Civilization/> 24 Sep 2018.

Cartwright, Mark. "Quetzalcoatl." *Ancient History Encyclopedia.* 1 Aug 2013. <https://www.ancient.eu/Quetzalcoatl/> 30 Nov 2019.

"Castor and Pollux." *The Columbia Encyclopedia,* 6th ed. *Encyclopedia.com.* <https://www.encyclopedia.com/literature-and-arts/classical-literature-mythology-and-folklore/folklore-and-mythology/castor-and-pollux> 23 Sep 2019.

"Central American Fer-De-Lance, Bothrops asper." *The Dallas World Aquarium.* <https://dwazoo.com/animal/central-american-fer-de-lance/> 21 Nov 2019.

Cheney, Mark F.. *Mark of the Jaguar, A Book of Mormon Adventure in the Land of the Maya.* Bloomington, IN, Author House, 2014.

"Cerro Rabón." *Beyond the Sump.* <https://www.beyondthesump.org/cerro-rabon> 22 Oct 2019.

"The Citadel and the Feathered Serpent Pyramid." *On the Road in Teotihuacan.* <https://www.ontheroadin.com/Mexico%20Archeology/Citadel%20and%20The%20Feathered%20Serpent%20Pyramid.htm> 17 Oct 2019.

Crowell, Angela. "Hebraisms in the Book of Mormon." *Recent Book of Mormon Developments: Articles from The Zarahemla Record.* Independence, MO; Zarahemla Research Foundation, 1984.

"Coatzacoalcos" *Wikipedia, the Free Encyclopedia.* <https://en.wikipedia.org/wiki/Coatzacoalcos> 8 Jul 2019.

Coe, Michael D. *The Maya,* 7th ed. New York: Thames & Hudson. 2005.

Coleman, Arlene. Graduate thesis. "The Construction of Complex A at La Venta, Tabasco, Mexico: A History of Buildings, Burials, Offerings, and Stone Monuments." Provo, Utah: Brigham Young University. Aug 2010. <https://www.academia.edu/11950743/The_Construction_of_Complex_A_at_La_Venta_Tabasco_Mexico_A_History_of_Building_Burials_Offerings_and_Stone_Monuments> 16 Aug 2019.

Coll, Fern. "Exploring the Teotihuacan Pyramids in Mexico." *Chimu Blog.* <http://search.pollicare.com/?t=1807&ap=1478616638660322&r=213807bde8e333aef66119f5815b63a2&hp=1> 16 Oct 2019.

Damrosch, David. *The Narrative Covenant: Transformations of Genre in the Growth of Biblical Literature.* San Francisco, CA: Harper and Row, 1987.

DeLong, Richard A. "Maya Glyphs May Identify Hill Cumorah." *The Witness, No. 67.* Independence, MO: Book of Mormon Foundation, Winter 1989.

Egal, Florent. "The Valley of Moses" *The Saudi Arabia Tourism Guide.* 5 Mar 2018. <http://www.saudiarabiatourismguide.com/tayeb-ism/> 23 Jan 2020.

"El Manati." *WikiVisually.* <https://wikivisually.com/wiki/El_Manat%C3%AD> 21 Nov 2019.

"English Translations of Plato's Atlantis Dialogues, Benjamin Jowett 1871." *Atlanta-Scout.* <https://www.atlantis-scout.de/atlantis_timaeus_critias.htm#-jowett> 10 Jul 2019.

Espindola, J.M., J.L. Macias, R.I. Tilling, and M.F. Sherida. *"Volcanic history of El Chichón Volcano (Chiapas, Mexico) during the Holocene, and its impact on human activity* (abstract)." Bulletin of Volcanology Vol. 62, No. 90. Jun 2000. <https://doi.org/10.1007/s004459900064> 30 May 2018.

Fackler, Martin. "After the Tsunami, Japan's Sea Creatures Crossed an Ocean." *The New York Times.* 28 Sep 2017. <https://www.nytimes.com/2017/09/28/science/tsunami-japan-debris-ocean.html> 3 Feb 2020.

Fell, Barry. *America B.C., Ancient Settlers in the New World.* New York: Pocket Books, 1976.

"Fernando de Alva Cortés Ixtlilxóchitl." *Archaeological and Historical Evidence.* <http://www.supportingevidences.net/fernando-de-alva-corts-ixtlilx/> 2 Oct 2019.

German, Dr. Senta. "Ziggurat of Ur." Khan Academy <https://www.khanacademy.org/humanities/ancient-art-civilizations/ancient-near-east1/sumerian/a/ziggurat-of-ur> 10 Sep 2019.

"'Ghost ship' from Japan tsunami spotted off Canada." *Thejournal.ie.* 26 Mar 2012. <https://www.thejournal.ie/ghost-ship-from-japan-tsunami-spotted-off-canada-396272-Mar2012/> 3 Feb 2020.

Glacquinta, Patricia, Ph.D. "Did the Mi'kmaq From Eastern Canada Write in Egyptian Hieroglyphics?" *Knitting It Together, Lost History, Mystery, and Yarns.* 5 Nov 2015.

Goetz, T. D. and S. G. Morley, translators. From the translation of Adrian Recinos. *Popol Vuh, The Sacred Book of the Ancient Quiché Maya.* Norman, OK: University of Oklahoma Press. 1950.

Grondine, E. P. *Re: The Sun of the Wind, a passage from the Historia Tolteca-Chichieca.* Forum: New World. 30 Apr 2017. <https://www.archaeologica.org/forum/search.php?keywords=precious+feathers&t=3853&sf=msgonly > Accessed 7 Feb 2019.

Grover, Jerry D.. *Sumerian Roots of Jaredite-Derived Names and Terminology in the Book of Mormon.* Provo, UT: Challex Scientific Publications. 2017.

Hays, J. Daniel. "Black Soldiers." *Bible Review,* Vol. 14, no. 4 Aug 1998.

Heren, Louis. *China's Three Thousand Years: The Story of a Great Civilization.* New York: Macmillan Publishing Company, 1974.

Heyworth, Robin. "History of Teotihuacan." *Uncovered History.* 13 Nov 2014. <https://uncoveredhistory.com/mexico/teotihuacan/history-of-teotihuacan/> 16 Oct 2019.

Hirsch, Emil G., et al. "Jehoiakim." *Jewish Encyclopedia.* 1906. <http://www.jewishencyclopedia.com/articles/8562-jehoiakim> 28 Dec 2019.

Hirsch, Emil G., et al. "Nebuchadnezzar." *Jewish Encyclopedia.* 1906. <http://www.jewishencyclopedia.com/articles/11407-nebuchadnezzar> 11 Oct 2019.

Hirst, K. Kris. "San Lorenzo (Mexico)" *Thought Co.* 7 Mar 2017. <https://www.thoughtco.com/san-lorenzo-mexico-olmec-172604> 16 Sep 2019.

Hoskisson, Paul Y., Brian M. Hauglid, and John Gee. "What's in a Name? Irreantum." *Journal of Book of Mormon Studies*, Vol. 11, No. 1, 2002.

Hunter, Milton R. and Thomas Stuart Ferguson. *Ancient America and the Book of Mormon.* Whitefish, MT: Literary Licensing LLC, 1950.

Jansen, Maarten and Gabina Aurora Pérez Jiménez. *Time and the Ancestors: Aztec and Mixtec Ritual Art.* Leiden, Netherlands; Brill Academic Pub., 2017.

Jarus, Owen. "Teotihuacan: Ancient City of Pyramids." *Live Science.* 20 Aug 2012. <https://www.livescience.com/22545-teotihuacan.html> 16 Oct 2019.

Kang, C. H. and E. R. Nelson. *The Discovery of Genesis: How the Truths of Genesis Were Found in the Chinese Language.* St. Louis, MO: Concordia Publishing House, 1979.

"King Herod the Great plans how to kill Jesus." *Bibleview.* <https://bibleview.org/en/bible/birthofjesus/angryherod/> 11 Oct 2019.

Kingsborough, Lord. *Antiquities of Mexico,* Vol. IX. London, Henry G. Bohn, York St., Covent Garden. 1848.

Kramer, S. N. "The 'Babel of Tongues': A Sumerian Version." *Journal of the American Oriental Society, Vol.* 88.1, 1968.

Kramer, S. N., Ph.D., and E. I. Gordon, Ph.D. "Ur," Microsoft® Encarta® Online Encyclopedia 2000. <http://autocww.colorado.edu/~toldy2/E64ContentFiles/ArchaeologyAndExcavations/Ur.html> 10 Sep 2019.

"Lamanai Belize." *Mayan Ruins.* <http://mayanruins.info/belize/lamanai-belize/> 26 Sep 2019.

Lemonick, Michael D. "Mystery of the Olmec." *Time.* 24 Jun 2001. <http://content.time.com/time/magazine/article/0,9171,136151,00.html> 24 Oct 2019.

León-Portilla, Miguel. *Pre-Columbian Literatures of Mexico.* Norman, University of Oklahoma Press, 1969.

The Library of History of Diodorus Siculus, Vol. III. Loeb Classical Library
edition, 1939. <http://penelope.uchicago.edu/Thayer/E/Roman/Texts/
Diodorus_Siculus/5B*.html> 17 Aug 2019.

Lindsey, Zack. "Unbounding the Past: Events in Ancient and Contemporary
Maya History for May" *IMS Explorer, Institute of Maya Studies*, Vol. 47,
No. 5, May 2019.

Ludlow, Daniel H., ed. "Book of Mormon Editions (1830–1981)"
Encyclopedia of Mormonism. New York, Macmillan Publishing Co.
Copyright, Brigham Young University, 1992.

MacWhorter, Alexander. "Tammuz and the Mound Builders" *The Galaxy*,
Vol. 14. Jul to Dec 1872. <https://books.google.com/books?id=cTG-
gAAAAMAAJ&pg=PA93&lpg=PA93&dq> 22 Sep 2018.

Maestri, Nicoletta. "Diego de Landa (1524–1579), Bishop and Inquisitor
of Early Colonial Yucatan." *ThoughtCo.* 8 Mar 2017. <https://www.
thoughtco.com/diego-de-landa-inquisitor-colonial-yucatan-171622> 30
Nov 2019.

Manzanilla, Linda R. "Teotihuacan: An Exceptional Multiethnic City in Pre-
Hispanic Central Mexico." *Center for Latin American Studies: UC Berkeley.*
15 April 2015. <https://clas.berkeley.edu/events/spring-2015/teotihuacan-ex-
ceptional-multiethnic-city-pre-hispanic-central-mexico> 9 Aug 2018.

Mathisen, David Warner. *The Case of the Micmac Hieroglyphs: a Powerful
Blow to Isolationist Theories.* The Mathisen Corollary. 13 Jul 2011.
<http://mathisencorollary.blogspot.com/2011/07/case-of-micmac-hiero-
glyphs-powerful.html> 23 Jun 2019.

"Mayan History (Part 42): Uaxactun." *Autodidact-adventures.* May 20,
2017. <https://autodidact-adventures.tumblr.com/post/160856793490/
mayan-history-part-42-uaxactun> 19 Oct 2019.

Minster, Christopher. "The Historic Olmec City of San Lorenzo"
ThoughtCo. 15 Jun 2019. <https://www.thoughtco.com/the-olmec-city-
of-san-lorenzo-2136302> 23 Nov 2019.

Muscato, Christopher. "Historical Chichimeca Peoples: Culture & History."
History, Culture & People of the Americas. <https://study.com/academy/
lesson/historical-chichimeca-peoples-culture-history.html> 1 Oct 2019.

Nibley, Hugh. *Lehi in the Desert and the World of the Jaredites.* Salt Lake City, UT: Bookcraft, 1952.

Normark, Johan (posted by). "The Last Stand at El Mirador?" Archaeological Haecceities. 17 Sep 2009. <https://haecceities.wordpress.com/2009/09/17/the-last-stand-at-el-mirador/> 5 Jul 2018.

O'Leary, Terry. "Book of Mormon Years." *The Witness,* No. 134. Independence, MO, Book of Mormon Foundation, Summer 2010.

"Olmec Civilization." *Crystallinks.com.* <https://www.crystalinks.com/olmec.html> 21 Nov 2019.

"On This Day in History: Spanish Priest Diego de Landa Burned the Sacred Books of Maya—On July 12, 1562." *Ancient Pages.* Jul 12, 2016. <http://www.ancientpages.com/2016/07/12/on-this-day-in-history-spanish-priest-diego-de-landa-burned-the-sacred-books-of-maya-on-july-12-1562/> 1 Oct 2019.

Phillips, Charles. *The Complete Illustrated History: Aztec & Maya.* NY: Metro Books. 2008.

Plunket, Patricia and Gabriela Uruñuela. "The archaeology of a Plinian eruption of the Popocatépetl volcano." *Geological Society, London, Special Publications.* 1 Jan 2000. <https://sp.lyellcollection.org/content/171/1/195> 17 Nov 2019.

Potter, George D. "A Candidate in Arabia for the 'Valley of Lemuel.'" *Book of Mormon Central.* 1999. <https://archive.bookofmormoncentral.org/content/new-candidate-arabia-"valley-lemuel"> 18 Sep 2019.

Potter, George and Richard Wellington. *Discovering the Lehi-Nephi Trail.* Unpublished manuscript. 2000. *Step by Step Through the Book of Mormon, First Nephi 16:23* <https://stepbystep.alancminer.com/node/2229 > 7 Jun 2018.

Praise, Frank, ed. *The Book of Calendars.* New York, Facts on File, Inc., 1982.

Pumpelly, Raphael, ed. *Explorations in Turkestan, Expedition of 1904: Prehistoric Civilizations of Anau, Origins, Growth, and Influence of Environment.* v. 2. Washington, D.C.: Carnegie Institution of

Washington. 1908. <https://books.google.com/books?id=74kzlWWnNO-QC&pg=PA286&lpg=PA286&dq> 20 May 1918.

Rank, Michael Scott, Editor. "Mayan Art of the Tattoo" *History on the Net.* <https://www.historyonthenet.com/mayan-art-of-the-tattoo/> 30 May 2018.

Ricks, Stephen D. and Dennis L. Largey, Editor. "Anti-Nephi-Lehi." *Book of Mormon Reference Companion.* Salt Lake City, UT: Deseret Book Company. 2003.

Roberts, David. "Secrets of the Maya: Deciphering Tikal." *Smithsonian.com.* Jul 2005. <https://www.smithsonianmag.com/history/secrets-of-the-maya-deciphering-tikal-2289808/> 16 Oct 2019.

Scott, Glenn A. *Voices from the Dust: New Light on an Ancient American Record.* Marceline, MO: Walsworth Publishing Co., 2002.

Schuster, Angela M. H. "Traders of the Maya." *Archaeology,* Vol. 62, No. 4. Jul/Aug 2009.

Selim, Jocelyn. "Chinatown, 1000 B.C." *Discover.* Feb 2000.

Shaw, Ben. "Punctuating the Bible." *The Aquila Report.* 1 Nov 2011. <https://www.theaquilareport.com/punctuating-the-bible/> 26 Oct 2019.

Siegel, Ethan. "'Volcanic Ash' Isn't Actually Ash." *Forbes.* 23 Aug 2018. <https://www.forbes.com/sites/startswithabang/2018/04/23/volcanic-ash-isnt-actually-ash/#244222de3dc1> 7 Oct 2018.

Simmons, Neil and Ray Treat. "Maya Hieroglyphs Point to the Book of Mormon," *The Zarahemla Record,* 19–21. Winter, Spring & Summer, 1983.

Simmons, Verneil W. *Peoples, Places and Prophecies.* Independence, MO: Zarahemla Research Foundation, 1986.

Spence, Michael W. *The Obsidian Industry of Teotihuacan.* American Antiquity Vol 32, No. 4, 1967.

Stern, Ephraim. "Phoenicia and Its Special Relationship with Israel." *Biblical Archaeology* Vol. 43, No. 6. Nov/Dec 2017.

Stephens, John L. *Incidents of Travel in Central America, Chiapas, and Yucatan.* NY: Harper & Brothers. 1841.

Sullivan, Timothy D., graduate thesis. "The Social and Political Evolution of Chiapa de Corzo, Chiapas, Mexico: An Analysis of Changing Strategies of Rulership in a Middle Formative Through Early Classic Mesoamerican Political Center" University of Pittsburgh, 2009.<https://www.researchgate.net/publication/292984759> 12 Dec 2017.

Szczepanski, Kallie. "The Yellow River's Role in China's History." *ThoughtCo.* 28 Jul 2019. <https://www.thoughtco.com/yellow-river-in-chinas-history-195222> 2 Jan 2020.

"Teotihuacan, The New World's First Great City." *Mexonline.com.* <http://www.mexonline.com/history-teotihuacan.htm> 17 Oct 2019.

Thesiger, William. *Arabian Sands.* London: Penguin Classics. 1959. <https://books.google.com/books?id=SH6crRdP9sUC&p> 28 Jul 2018.

Torquemada, Juan. *Monarquia Indiana.* Spain, 1723. Quoted in: P. De Roo. *History of America Before Columbus, Vol. 1, American Aborigines.* Philadelphia: J. B. Lippincott Co., 1900. <https://books.google.com/books?id=oudBAAAAIAAJ&pg=PA424&lpg=PA424&dq> 7 Sep 2018.

Traxler, Loa P. and Robert J. Sharer, ed. *The Origins of Maya States.* Philadelphia, University of Pennsylvania Press: 2016.

Treat, Virgil A. and Robert F. Johnon. "Saudi Arabia Investigation Report (IR) SA-59." *United State Department of the Interior Geological Survey.* 1968. <https://pubs.usgs.gov/of/1968/0277/report.pdf> 24 Jan 2020.

"Volcano Hazards Program." *U.S. Geological Survey.* 20 Dec 1999. <https://volcanoes.usgs.gov/Imgs/Jpg/SoufHills/32424296-060_caption.html> 30 May 2018.

Vulich, Nick. *History Bytes: 37 People, Places, and Events That Shaped American History.* Digital History Project. Lulu.com. 2015. <https://books.google.com/books?id=iNgNCgAAQBAJ&pg=PA3&lpg=PA3&dq=%22in+the+deep+off+Africa+is+an+island+of+considerable+size> 10 Jul 2019.

Weldon, Roy. *Other Sheep.* Independence, MO: Herald Publishing House, 1958.

"What Do We Know about Lamanai?" *Lamanai Archaeology Project.* <https://lamanai.org.uk/index.html> 26 Sep 2019.

Whaley, Derek, ed. "Spearthrower Owl, King of Teotihuacán." *Dynastology.* 9 Jun 2012. <http://dynastology.blogspot.com/2012/06/spearthrower-owl-king-of-teotihuacan.html> 16 Oct 2019.

Whitlock, Robin. "Discovery of Hidden Mayan Stela and Panels Give Hints to the Importance of History in the Preclassical Period." *Ancient Origins.* 23 Jul 2015. <https://www.ancient-origins.net/news-history-archaeology/discovery-hidden-mayan-stela-and-panels-give-hints-importance-history-020453> 23 Oct 2019.

Wu, X. J., W. Liu, and C. J. Bae. "Craniofacial Variation Between Southern and Northern Neolithic and Modern Chinese." *International Journal of* Osteoarchaeology, Vol. 22. Wiley Online Library. 22 Jul 2010. <https://pdfs.semanticscholar.org/1dbe/d653578fc458d-c291af872725d323db0bb1c.pdf> 15 Nov 2019.

"Xia Dynasty—Ancient China's First Dynasty." *China Highlights.* < https://www.chinahighlights.com/travelguide/china-history/the-xia-dynasty.htm > 20 Nov 2019.

ABOUT THE AUTHOR

I grew up in Davenport, Iowa. After graduating from high school, I attended Graceland College (now Graceland University) in Lamoni, Iowa. I received an A.A. degree in 1963. After five years at Central Missouri State College (now University of Central Missouri) in Warrensburg, Missouri, I completed undergraduate majors in biology, geology, and psychology/education with minors in general science and mathematics. I was awarded membership in the Beta Beta Beta Biological Honor Society and Sigma Zeta Honorary Science Society. I received a B.S. in Education in 1965 and an M.S. degree in biology in 1968.

As this was during the Vietnam era, draft boards for military service were in full force. I chose to join the Navy, although, at that time, I had never seen an ocean. With my educational background, I was offered the opportunity to become an aerospace physiologist along with a direct commission to Lieutenant Junior Grade (O-2). I accepted and remained in the Navy for twenty years. Because of that specialty, all of my duty stations were in the states. After twenty years, I retired as a Commander (0-5) in the Medical Service Corps.

Before retiring from the Navy, I updated my teaching credentials. I was then able to teach in the public school system of Virginia Beach, Virginia. I taught eighth-grade general science for four years before moving to a high school where I taught biology and earth science for sixteen years. I was the science department chair for the last nine years.

After retiring again in 2008, I have been able to pursue my passion for researching both church history and the Book of Mormon.

I have been married for over fifty years to the former Patricia J. Boorjian. We have two sons. We are currently living in St. Augustine, Florida.

Terrence J. O'Leary